THE OWNER-BUILT LOG HOUSE

THE
OWNER-BUILT
LOG HOUSE

LIVING IN HARMONY WITH YOUR ENVIRONMENT

B. ALLAN MACKIE

FIREFLY BOOKS

A FIREFLY BOOK

Published by Firefly Books Ltd. 2001

National Library of Canada Cataloguing-in-Publication Data

Mackie, B. Allan (Bernard Allan), 1925–
   The owner-built log house: living in harmony with your
environment

ISBN 1-55297-548-7 (pbk)
ISBN 1-55297-549-5 (bound)

1. Log cabins – Design and construction – Amateurs' manuals.
I. Title

TH4840.M318   2001   690'.837   C2001-930721-7

U.S. Cataloging-in-Publication Data
   (Library of Congress Standards)

Mackie, B. Allan.
   The owner-built log house: living in harmony with your
environment / B. Allan Mackie. – 1st ed.
[232] p.: ill.: photos. (some col.);   cm.
Includes bibliographic references and index.
Summary: A step-by-step guide to building a log house.

ISBN 1-55297-548-7 (pbk.)
ISBN 1-55297-549-5 (bound)

1. House construction – Amateurs' manuals.   2. Wooden-
frame houses – Design and construction.   3. Log cabins –
Design and construction.   I. Title

690.837   21   2001

Published in Canada in 2001
by Firefly Books Ltd.
3680 Victoria Park Avenue
Willowdale, Ontario
Canada M2H 3K1

Published in the United States in 2001
by Firefly Books (U.S.) Inc.
P.O. Box 1338, Ellicott Station
Buffalo, New York
USA 14205

Design: Counterpunch/Linda Gustafson
Editor: Charis Cotter
Photographs: Nadina Mackie Jackson, Daizen Log-Tech, B. Allan Mackie,
Anand Maharaj and Sabine Mohr

Printed and bound in Canada by Friesens, Altona, Manitoba

*The Publisher acknowledges the financial support of the Goverment of Canada through
the Book Publishing Industry Development Program for its publishing activities.*

Acknowledgments

Nothing much is ever accomplished alone and that is how it should be. Work, any kind of work, is a lot more fun when others are involved. Making this book has been a lot more fun because of the other people involved – indeed, without them it would not have been done at all.

I would therefore like to thank editor Charis Cotter and designer Linda Gustafson for their expertise and good nature, and my publisher, Firefly Books, especially Michael Worek, for his patience and generosity. I also wish to thank Dai and Mike of Daizen Log-Tech for their help and unfailing support, and Mr. Kim, who came all the way from Korea and may just be the most wonderful guy on earth.

A local log builder, Paul Pitkanin, was a great help, as have been the neighbors at Shanty Lake, the McEwan families: Charlie, Peter, Jim and Ted. Thanks also to the photographer Anand Maharaj of Toronto, who likes to take pictures of people.

Finally, my heartfelt thanks go to my daughter Nadina and my son-in-law Fraser Jackson, for their hard work and their ongoing support and enthusiasm for this book, the houses at Shanty Lake and my many other projects.

Metric Measurements

Metric measurements are the standard used by the building industry everywhere in the world that I go to teach, with the exception of the United States. Therefore, all measurements in this book are expressed metrically. A metric conversion table can be found in the Appendix. Where the size of a tool is given in mm or kg, the equivalent is given in inches or pounds in the text.

TABLE OF CONTENTS

Allan, Nadina and Jake at Shanty Lake, 2000.

My father, B. Allan Mackie, is widely known as the man who resurrected the ancient profession of building with logs and brought it into the twenty-first century as a practical, environmentally friendly method of creating a home. His first book, *Building With Logs,* became the standard reference manual for people building their own log homes, and his school, the B. Allan Mackie School of Log Building in Prince George, British Columbia, was the first source of complete instruction for professional log builders. He is the founder of the Canadian Log Building Association and has personally provided the continuing professional example that has successfully revived this centuries-old skill throughout much of the world.

Allan is always genuinely surprised that people want to hear about his life. While it is tempting for me to make singsong lists of his many accomplishments – rancher, builder, sailor, writer, artist, teacher, filmmaker – it really is his searching spirit coupled with an endlessly inventive and supremely practical mind that

has led him down so many trails, usually alone, but at the same time inspiring thousands of like-minded people.

I see that my father, even and perhaps especially when in complete solitude, lives as a performer. It is a favorite request of his students to have him cut a notch completely with the axe rather than the chainsaw. From the rough cut to the razor-sharp curve and smooth interior of the finished notch, he can still do it from start to finish without stopping, the bright axe biting cleanly along the pencil line of the scribe mark. Watching him do it last winter, I asked how he could even see the line. He said that he has never looked at the line. Students ask how he cuts the line, and he says that he has no intention of hitting anywhere other than the line. The moment he launches the axe into its curve of motion, he releases all self-doubt and trusts himself to know exactly where the line is. He said at that moment he is not guiding the direction of the axe but instead following it.

I have seen my father carve homesteads out

of three tracts of wilderness: first when I was a happily oblivious toddler at the Silloep Hills Ranch in northern British Columbia; then as a sullenly oblivious teenager at the first B. Allan Mackie School of Log Building in Prince George; and now as a reflective forty-two-year-old, trying to keep pace with a man who is supposed to be a senior citizen as he builds a new home at Shanty Lake in Ontario.

This is the man who built my cradle, pulled tools from his pocket to repair the flickering overhead lights in the hospital delivery room when my brother Keith was being born, and forty years later, made some delicate repairs to my bassoon that allowed me to continue an important rehearsal. It is part of his nature to have never imposed his vocation on me, and though I regret not having my father's rare skills, his attitude has allowed me to become proficient in a métier far removed from his own.

B. Allan Mackie describes himself as having been a solitary and thoughtful child, prone to getting in trouble for taking things apart (though he quickly learned to put them back together). He was born on October 16, 1925, into a family who had arrived a generation earlier from Norfolk, England. They settled and established a farm on the rolling prairie near Battleford, Saskatchewan. Though there was much hard work in breaking and farming the prairie sod, there was also time for music, books and art. Allan said that they had a big enough collection of books to refer to it as a library, and any time not spent working was devoted to devouring books. His mother had been a teacher before her marriage with special interests in math, history and Latin. She was also an accomplished contralto and his father was an organist. Occasionally all five children were lined up to memorize and practise their hymns, though my father says there was more complaining than singing. It is one of his better-kept secrets that he can play the guitar and sing many a ballad.

He left home in 1943 at the age of seventeen to join the Royal Canadian Air Force, then transferred to the Canadian Army to become a fully-trained paratrooper in the legendary First Canadian Parachute Battalion. He was en route overseas when peace came. Demobilized, he enrolled at the University of British Columbia, but the overcrowded campus soon wore thin, and Allan switched to a government-sponsored carpentry course, which suited him well at the time. He then went back to Battleford and built a new frame house on the Mackie family homestead.

Allan's boyhood dream was to be a cowboy. He struck off for the Cariboo country of north-central British Columbia where he worked in logging camps and on ranches. He's proud to have ridden as a cowboy in the Anahim Stampede, and on one of the last cattle drives from Anahim Lake overland through the mountains to Williams Lake.

During a visit to his parents, then living in retirement in Victoria, British Columbia, he met and married Mary Mackie in 1952. There was a clear understanding from the beginning that life for my mother wasn't going to be humdrum or even comfortable. They soon sold their small house in Victoria and headed into the British Columbia interior, buying a beautiful two-hundred-acre farm with one-half mile of lakefront on François Lake. Allan became a B.C. Forest Ranger and took charge of the local ranger station. It was in 1955,

Allan and Nadina at the Silloep Hills ranch, 1962.

while on one of his many tours of duty in and around the Tweedsmuir Park region, that he discovered what would become the Silloep Hills Ranch: one thousand acres of natural grassland with a sweeping view of Nadina Mountain.

Allan built the Silloep Hills ranch from scratch, while my mother helped with all the attendant tasks of homesteading as well as caring for my brother and me, two babies in diapers (running water came later). She supplemented their income by writing stories about their daily lives for the *Family Herald* magazine.

They worked hard for six years, finishing the big ranch house and building up a good herd of Hereford and Shorthorn mixed cattle. They then reluctantly made the decision to leave the remote ranch, feeling that it was important to get good schooling for their children. Our family went to the peaceful coastal town of Powell

River, where my father had a job supervising the log-sorting grounds of Macmillan Bloedel.

During the turbulent sixties, my parents were very busy with interests that pulled them in different directions and their marriage was strained. Allan returned to the University of British Columbia, this time to take a Vocational Teaching degree. Each summer he returned to the Silloep Hills ranch to help the tenants bring in the hay. My mother enrolled at Simon Fraser University to work on a history degree.

Allan took a teaching job in Williams Lake, British Columbia, then an even more interesting one at Fort Smith in the Northwest Territories, during which he canoed the length of the Mackenzie River to Inuvik. Allan and Mary almost separated at this point, but chose to set aside their differences for the sake of their children.

In 1970 they made a new start in the interior town of Prince George, British Columbia, where Allan joined the faculty of the College of New Caledonia and began teaching log-building as an Adult Education night school course. It was so popular that he convinced the college to offer it as a regular, eight-month vocational course. But the heavy demand from so many students outside the college's mandated region signaled to Allan and Mary that an innovative solution was needed. The over-flow enrolments led to the creation of the first B. Allan Mackie School of Log Building, established on the Mackies' own ten-acre homesite. *Building With Logs* evolved from the notes for these courses. Mary was the editor, typesetter, publisher and in charge of all the distribution and mailing for the next two decades. While they were developing the publishing business, they built a log home and log-building school in the woods near Square Lake, about thirty miles from Prince George. From this followed six other books and eventually, a nine-part video series.

In the 1980s, a student named Kyu Hoshino came from Japan to invite Allan to teach courses in Japan each summer. This led to the extension of Allan's teaching career throughout the world. He now teaches annually in Canada, the United States, Japan, Korea, Germany, Sweden and Romania. He immensely enjoys the paradoxes of his life that take him from his solitary computer in the middle of the woods to demonstrating hand-cut notches in the middle of Tokyo.

In 1990, my father began work on a series of videos demonstrating how to build your own log home. With his usual stubbornness, determination and independence, Allan undertook every aspect of the videomaking from the filming to the editing. He made several changes of computer systems until he found exactly the right combination of camera and editing equipment for both image and sound. The series ended up taking far longer that he originally anticipated, partly because he took several months off to finish outfitting his thirty-four-foot sailboat and sail to Hawaii and back. Upon his return, he reapplied himself to filming and editing, using his new high-tech skills to finish the video project in a series of sixteen-hour days.

In 1996 my parents decided without regrets to go their separate ways after forty-four volatile but productive years of marriage. The decision to part company was final, providing them both with yet another new frontier to cross at a time of life when most people opt to bicker in comfort.

Mary kept the Pender Island home, where they had lived together since 1984, and Allan moved to Ontario to be closer to me and my family. And in 2001, Allan had a visit from his eldest Australian grandson, Tom. My brother Keith emigrated to Australia while still a teenager, and is now a furniture builder there. Tom was able to visit his grandfather in a setting that truly reflects his life: deep in the snow-covered forest, snug in a house built by his own hands.

My father moved to Ontario from British Columbia just over two years ago. In that time, he has bought land on a beautiful remote lake, built a long road over difficult terrain, finished one house as well as the walls and foundations of another, completed his nine-part educational video series, spent five months teaching throughout the world and finished this book that you now hold in your hands. He also helped us to move, makes repairs to our Victorian brick house and babysits his three-year-old grandson while my husband and I play in concerts. He makes a mean beef stew and helps wash the dishes. And when I visit his forest home, I have the indescribable joy of waking up in a log house that my father built, stirring my earliest memories of happiness and well being.

At the age of seventy-five, Allan still relishes the demands and the unpredictability of living independently in hard nature. He enumerates the difficulties with an animation that borders on passion. Here he describes a trip to Parry Sound on February 14, 2000:

"I'm not a recluse (despite appearances) so I think I should go to town today – need things like orange juice and maybe a piece of fish, getting a little tired of rolled oats and rice.

then wait half an hour for it to warm up by the fire.

In the meantime, put an electric space heater under the truck then put fiberglass insulation behind the engine and all around then cover it all with a tarp. Shovel snow onto the tarp so it won't blow away. Drag the generator outside again and start it quick then plug in the heater. Fill the fuel tank carefully. Now go inside and have breakfast while the oil heats up in the truck; this will take about one hour. The truck's starter doesn't work too well but finally hooks in and the old girl starts. Rip off all the shrouding and shut down the generator. Check the wood stove and load any last minute items into the truck, then off to the neighbor's house where my van awaits.

I now have to plug in the diesel van and wait another hour for it to warm up a little. The glow plugs don't work and the starter won't make contact, so open the hood and have Charlie standing by with a can of starting fluid. I crawl under and short the solenoid across from the positive lead of the battery. This will crank the engine and Charlie gives it a shot of ether. Engine roars to life as I duck the shower of sparks from the jump-start maneuver. Now I'm off to town to get a box of orange juice. If I don't make a mistake and shut the engine off while I go into the grocery store, I should be back before dark. No, I'm not a recluse, but sometimes it seems like a reasonable alternative."

Nadina Mackie Jackson
Toronto, March 6, 2001

Allan and Jake at Shanty Lake, 2000.

Town is only forty kilometers away, no big deal despite the cost of fuel, but there are a few things to consider. I ploughed the driveway three days ago, all 3.3 kilometers of it, and should still be able to get the truck through the ten centimeters of new snow. But I will have to get up before daylight and drag in the Makita generator because it won't start outside when it is -20° F. Drag it through the door

The kind of house that sits easily on my mind is not necessarily designed just to be efficient for space, heat and materials. It would also be carefully planned to take into account comfort, movement, sunlight and friends. The setting, as I imagine it, would be among tall trees and the house would be low to the ground and inconspicuous. There would be space and sunlight in the front of the house, and it would be situated far from the road, with a narrow and unimposing driveway. The entrance would allow easy access: ground level or near to it.

Inside the door, the first thing you see would be the fireplace and the next thing would be some aspect of the kitchen or dining room, to add to the atmosphere of welcome and warmth. This is not a commercial place and a visitor would also be a friend. He might sit casually at the counter stools or at the dining-room table, or come deeper into the house and relax with the books and soft light of the living room.

This house is built for me and my friends, both inside and outside the house. My friends are the many people who may come and share their valuable time with me and also the patient trees, with whom I feel such a close bond and to whom I owe so very much.

Sketch of Ardea, the big house at Shanty Lake.
I named it after the great blue heron who lives nearby.
Ardea is the Latin name for his species.

CHAPTER 1

THE PURPOSE IN BUILDING A LOG HOUSE

A PERSONAL LOG HOUSE

From the dawn of human history, people have used trees and rocks to build the shelters they needed. By the time tools had developed enough to be able to shape and refine stone, men would already have had tools capable of shaping wood. Therefore, wood is among our oldest building materials. And I believe that everyone in any pre-history community would have been familiar with the ways of log building. It would be a skill as important as hunting, food gathering and fighting. This was not a matter of fashion for them, as it is for us. It was a matter of survival. How welcome, and what a blessing those shelters must have been! And from those ancestral feelings of gladness toward the tree-walls which protected them, come our own feelings for log buildings.

When I first started to teach the skills of timber building in 1970, I was not fully aware of this phenomenon. It sometimes annoyed me that people interrupted my work to tell me the "only way" to build with logs, when I

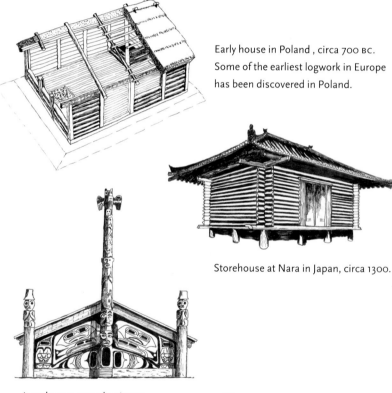

Early house in Poland , circa 700 BC. Some of the earliest logwork in Europe has been discovered in Poland.

Storehouse at Nara in Japan, circa 1300.

Longhouse reproduction at Kitwanga, British Columbia.

Early Ontario settler's house, circa 1840.

B. Allan Mackie residence, School of Log Building, Prince George, British Columbia, 1973.

could see that their information was the product of fantasy or faulty folklore. I would try to change their minds, so that if they tried to build in the future, they would build better houses. But often they wouldn't listen. They would go away angry and hurt. Then, slowly, I began to realize that they were coming to me to share a dream. It was the dream I should discuss with them, in its proper place: why we love log buildings. Later, when their minds were resolved to build, I could teach the correct methods for building.

When I built the Kerry Street House in Prince George, British Columbia, in 1973, one of my students was totally inexperienced. At one point we needed him to pass a sledge-hammer from the second floor to the roof structure we were framing and he didn't even know how to tie it to the rope we lowered to him. I became increasingly frustrated by my inability to explain this verbally. Finally, he defused the situation by falling off the building.

The next year, when I was in the Eastern Townships of the Province of Quebec, he contacted me and asked if I would like to see the house he had built. I did and saw that he had done an excellent job. I have learned a lot from students and I learned right then to respect everyone's dreams, no matter how impractical they may seem.

There are many dreams within the big dream of living in a log house. One is for young people: they see their energies invested in the beginning of their worldly estate. They see themselves with the wind in their hair and the sweat on their foreheads glinting in the sunlight as they express their joyful hopes for a good future through hard work. The best of dreams! Others, like doctors and teachers, see a health dimension. Carpenters, construction workers and accountants also seek to cure something in their work lives that is not satisfying them. Many see the log building as merely possible: something that looks easy that they can build without a heavy mortgage debt. All of these dreams are worthy of respect. And I believe that all of these dreams arise from our deep ancestral needs to feel again the sheltering warmth of the logs, to smell their fragrance, and to know that within those tree-walls, we are safe.

All these students had much to learn. They had to learn everything! If pre-screening had been allowed, my students would never have passed the entry requirements. But I knew from the beginning that all I needed in students were their dreams and their determination. So I have never refused entry to a student.

And so, for these reasons, the log house becomes the most personal house. It is not only a true reflection of the builder, but it also binds the builder to nature because of the materials he uses. He cannot dominate those trees, and say, "There! I will force you into this space, whether you like it or not!" It just won't work. The builder must enter into a dialogue with the trees and discover their essence: how they might fit, are they big enough, small enough and so on. When the builder and the tree understand what is needed, they work together in harmony, each aiding the other. This builds an intense appreciation and love of building.

ALL BY YOURSELF

You're never all by yourself as long as you have the ancestral dream. This reassures you that many others, just like you, have built their own log homes; therefore, you can too.

In actual practice, you're never really alone. To be independent does not mean that only you must do every bit of work, little or large. This is not a competition. You will find that another person, or your whole family, or a dedicated group will stand by to help you. Do as much as possible by yourself because this provides you with a single-minded purpose. For example, if a contractor is involved, a new purpose is added: his purpose may be profit, or convenience in his work schedule, or experimentation using YOUR log house. Be aware of that and keep your own purpose clearly in mind.

You'll know very early that the real reason you need a log house is to heal or strengthen your soul by providing a true place for your heart to touch (ever so gently) nature, to which we are all connected. If you believe this, as I do myself, then you will agree that it's necessary to experience as fully as possible the hard work, the sweat and blisters, the worry, the thrills, the hopes and the pride of accomplishment in your new log home. If you allow someone else to do much of this work, you will give away part of that wonderful opportunity to stand close to your ancestors. You will feel, too late, that you have been robbed of your chance to

bond with the nature of the experience. But if you perform most of the work all by yourself you come that much closer to realizing your goal of working in harmony with nature

One group of workers belongs with you: your family. For they, too, wish to stand close to your shared ancestors, and to experience the log house as you do. The days you spend together working the wood will always be with you.

Can you, one small person (even with a family of helpers), expect to build a log house to a good standard of quality? My answer is "Yes you can," even though there are big logs to be lifted, logs you cannot budge. There are dangers from the machinery, from the sharp tools, the unfamiliar heights, the weight of the logs, even the costs. But still I say, "Yes, you can build a log house all by yourself." Many have done so: thousands of people. Some were in their mid-seventies; some were children. Men and women alike, they built with logs and in the process built up their inner strengths. You will, of course, need those strengths as the months go by.

FOR THE LOVE OF BUILDING

There are many beautiful building materials in the world. The best of these are natural materials: wood, stone and mud brick. The best material to use depends on what part of the planet you're on. Mud brick of adobe, for example, is ideal in those hot, treeless regions where the soil can be baked. But I am Canadian, and trees are my natural material. I offer two definitions: natural house logs are from trees that are modified only by hand-held tools. Lumber is from trees that are modified by large power machines.

Let us go deeper into our dream log house now, and ask ourselves why we want to use natural logs in construction when modern technology provides us with so many easy choices.

There are three main reasons for using natural logs in construction. First, a log house is one of the most aesthetically satisfying in which to live. Logs bring the world of nature back into our lives in a way that becomes ever more necessary to our survival. There is a deep sense of peace to be had from living in a house made from natural trees. No stripped, chipped, cooked, compressed, treated or otherwise manufactured product of industrial technology can give us such an awareness of each living tree, just as it once stood.

You, as the builder, will remember long after the house is completed, whether a tree had few limbs or many because of where it grew. You'll know how it looked as it fell to the ground. A scar may remind you of the day the log was skidded to the loading site. The length of time it took you to build will be recorded in the faint darkening of the rising walls as they become drier and less easy to peel. You will remember a log that chased you down the skids and one that resisted mightily before it was subdued and fitted into place. The scrubbing, oiling, and perhaps varnishing will warm the colors and highlight the textures of the new walls – revealing curves, limb lines, the lacework of bark beetles or the claw marks of a bear – all signs of nature to be saved and treasured.

Finally, there is a growing understanding of all vegetation having consciousness. I accept

that view, and I believe it accounts for that intense feeling of peace and thankfulness which permeates a natural, carefully built log home. I leave it with you to consider what response the living spirit of a tree must feel when it is put to rest as part of your well-loved household.

The family that builds a log house knows their home as a work of art. They can savor its unique qualities better than anyone else. None but the log house provides its own sweet incense of sap and resin. Solid timber walls have an acoustic quality that makes music sound richer. Harsh household clatter does not strike, echo and bounce as it does from plaster surfaces. The natural brown earth tones are restful to the eye. Above all, there is a quality of snug security in the fortress-thick walls. This may come from tradition, log construction being old and honored in history. A log building ties that time-tested tradition into our uncertain present, giving a welcome sense of continuity and stability.

The second advantage of log construction is durability. With a good foundation to protect the building from the composting urge of the earth, and a wide overhang on the roof to shelter against rain and snow soaking the walls, the log building will rival concrete and stone in its long life. In style, the log building has an amazing durability. The pressures of fashion have never succeeded in making a log building look outdated. It is in timeless good taste whether it is a simple building or one of the dramatic 20th-century designs. Logs have an innate harmony with the landscape as long as they are used with dignity and with care.

Third, log construction is the only contemporary construction method that enables an individual to exchange labor and ingenuity, rather than cash and a mortgage debt, for a home to be proud of.

My first home was built on the shores of Francois Lake in 1953 for a total cash outlay of $200. It was 700 square feet and the only purchased items were glass, roofing, spar varnish and rough lumber. The rest was accomplished with a good deal of innovating, trading, scrounging, and neighborly co-operation – all activities which are still permissible in many parts of the world. But where the use of logs as a building material requires not only the purchase and delivery of all materials, but also the hiring of builders, the log house will be as costly as frame or masonry construction. This should not deter the family able to afford what pleases them most. And savings will occur both in heating and air conditioning as well as the low cost of building maintenance over the centuries.

Building with logs does require hard work but it is healthy, pleasant work that is not at all beyond the strength of most families, as long as it is undertaken at a pace that permits full appreciation of the process as a once-in-a-lifetime experience.

The Ecological House

What is ecology? Ecology is the science of plants and animals in relation to their environment. For a great and increasing number of these plants and animals, this relationship is now fully explained with one word: extinct.

This is not a new occurrence in history. Even before the extinction of the dinosaurs, species were being obliterated by environmental change. Natural environmental change is beyond our ability to control, just as it was beyond the ability of the dinosaurs and mastodons to cope with the sudden disruption of their world. What is significant is that we are inflicting artificial change on the earth's environment, change that has the potential to include us in that list of extinct species. This is not a condemnation all of our activities, because many are positive and progressive. Fishing is a great and honorable activity, but drift net fishing is a terrible exploitation of our ecology. Logging is a great and honorable activity, but clear-cut logging devastates large areas of environmentally sensitive sites.

The subject is vast and complex. What it tells us is how careful we must be in building with logs. Done well, we will harvest and preserve at optimum usefulness: this is our goal. Our responsibility is specifically to build an ecologically compatible log house. By this, I mean a house that will not disturb or damage the relationship of plants and animals to the environment.

Ideally, no living trees would be cut; the only wood material available for heat and building would be deadwood. This seems like a strange and impossible objective, yet for many millions of years, this was the case. Because our forebears lacked the means to utilize standing trees, we became the inheritors of this vast resource. This has been our great good luck and we have squandered this wealth like immature children inheriting the family estate. We are looting the planet.

Trees are felled on the steep mountain slopes of British Columbia in vast clear-cut areas because this is the cheapest way to do it. The soil and foliage wash into the streams, rivers and

B. Allan Mackie residence, François Lake, British Columbia, 1953.

"while the radioactivity may put individual plants and animals at greater risk of cancer or deformity, this effect is outweighed at the population level by the advantage of not having people around." This indicates that from an environmental perspective, we are very poor citizens.

The first step then, in building our ecologically acceptable house, is to obtain the required logs without disrupting the plants and animals within the associated environment. Trees for a log house should be sound, straight and of a uniform size and shape. At one time, these could be found scattered throughout a suitable location in the forest, marked, carefully felled and skidded, most often with horses, to the building or loading site. This was the way we did it when I first started building log houses in 1947 and for the next 25 years. Such a process is still possible in unique situations where there are tracts of private forest available; otherwise logs are purchased to specification, from a logging company. This is necessarily the case if you have to import logs, but now we have fallen right into the same rut and we are contributing to the destruction of the forest environment.

There is no easy answer to this. To say, "Where these logs come from is not my problem," is untrue. No matter how far removed you are from this forest, you will still be deprived of trees. We will all eventually find ourselves little better off than the other creatures of the earth who watch with incomprehension as the air turns to poison and the water rises over their homes.

As a builder, there are presently two things you can do to help. One, insist on bona fide information that part of the purchase money for the logs is directed to reforestation, and two,

into the ocean. Rocks and ground soil that have not seen direct sunlight for millions of years now bake in the sun or wash away during the runoff. The trees are dragged to the roadsides, loaded onto great trucks and hauled to the beach, then through the sorting ground and on to the mills. They eventually reach the print shop and become comic books or junk mail to be directly turned into waste.

We all realize that it would be difficult to abruptly reverse this practice. We are locked into so many systems of waste and pointless production that change has to be gradual. But we would all be so much better off if we could redirect our activities. Starting right now, we must begin to set aside ever larger tracts of the earth's surface, including the oceans and the plains as well as the mountain tops. They need to be reserved from human intrusion to allow the earth, the water and the air to heal. It is noteworthy that as I write, scientists examining the exclusion zone surrounding the worst nuclear accident to date, the 1986 disaster at Chernobyl, find the plant and animal population thriving. Clive Cookson, of the *Japan Sun Times*, reported on October 30, 2000, that, join the worldwide effort to eliminate waste and exploitation from the forests and oceans.

Once you have located a supply of logs in as environmentally peaceful a manner as possible, look to your building location. Many houses are built where no house should be and on this ever-more crowded planet, the choice becomes increasingly limited. I have lived on an island that at one time was covered with huge Douglas fir and red cedar trees. Now it is largely covered with houses and any remaining big trees have to come down because, with the extensive clearings, the big trees are no longer wind-firm and become dangerous.

If possible, place your building gently within the landscape. Work by hand if possible, remove only the trees within the foundation's perimeter and care for those that are close to fills or excavations. This was done when we built the first house on Kerry Street in Prince George, British Columbia. The excavation was made with care that no trees were injured and the house was placed by hand so that clearings for machines were not needed. All the trees that were originally on the site are still there. In the front, where we needed to use approximately one-and-a-half meters of fill, the new owner found planks at the base of the trees. He was distressed, believing that they had been carelessly abandoned. As he began to remove them, he discovered that we had carefully placed the planks so that the roots of the trees (which were now much deeper in the ground) would not be suffocated while they became acclimatized to their new condition. The trees are still healthy.

Build by hand. I am aware that this is an idea that finds little support in today's industrial world, but as I have done many times before, I must insist that it is realistic. I do not object to chainsaws; they do a great deal of work for the amount of fuel that they burn. But this is a personal log house we are building and the clear measured ring of a good axe is far more acceptable than the stench of burning oil. Take delight in this skill and the acquiring of it. I have found that a house reflects the care and love that was expended on it: this is its true value. There is no better way to approach this true value than to work with hand tools, to work with skill and to work with respect.

So let us begin this discussion of how to build with logs knowing it to be truly a discussion, for there are always different ways to do each task. Every axe-man will find many new answers of his own, because a good part of the exercise of log building is that of the imagination. This is part of the craft. It is what helps to make each house unique and it is what makes each house both a work of art and the embodiment of a dream.

Kerry Street house. Built in Prince George, British Columbia, in 1973. This was the first log house I built that addressed all the requirements of a modern dwelling.

SHANTY LAKE

A NEW HOUSE

The beaver dam at Shanty Lake.

Shanty Lake is a mile-long bulge in a small unnamed creek that is searching its way through forty miles of forest and swamp to join Georgian Bay in the vicinity of Parry Sound in North Central Ontario. It could be considered remote by today's standards but it isn't really. I have to build and maintain my own three miles of road; I will have to supply my own electricity. Running water is the thing that washes out the road when the beavers vote to enlarge their territory.

It's the kind of place I like. It is also the result of a year-long search of Ontario within the radius of a three-hour drive to Toronto for just such a place. Why this place? Why here in the Ontario bush?

From my perspective it would be easy to claim a number of good and noble reasons to answer those questions, such as – let's see: 1) I am investigating the challenges encountered by the early settlers; 2) I am researching the possibilities of a modern-day homestead; 3) I wish to demonstrate a realistic choice in self-determination; and 4) I want to see how tough I am.

None of the above are true or even close. The fact is, I am seventy-five years old and I am doing exactly what I want to do and have wanted to do all of my life. What a wonderful experience! What a wonderful country in which this is possible and what wonderful support I've received from neighbors and friends around the world, whose observations have been patient, understanding, constructive and sometimes amused.

I have been building log buildings most of my life. Not professionally: professional log building only came into existence in the 1970s after I had already started teaching this skill to so many young people who were, and still are, ready to run with it. But nearly all my life I have been building log houses for myself, as places to live.

I like to live near the edge and to experience the reality of every occasion in which I am privileged to take part. In the process I have learned to do many things and I consider it another great privilege to be able to share that experience with others on occasion. I live and work at the edge of isolation. If I make one step west, I am on the highway; one step east and I have miles and miles of uninhabited wilderness.

Shanty Lake in winter.

So I am building again, at Shanty Lake. I am going to make myself comfortable and warm within this environment. I am going to do this without destroying anything and I am going to do my best to co-exist with my immediate neighbors: the beaver, raccoon, bear, wolves, deer, moose and the group of other old guys who have a hunt camp just down the road.

The beaver are the immediate challenge. They are determined to flood the shoreline. This flooding will create a ring of dead trees around the lake and the resulting vegetation in the water will eliminate the fish. One avenue is to leave the beaver alone. They will use up their food supply, become diseased and disappear. This they can accomplish a little

Shanty Lake in summer.

faster than human populations do, but it will still take too long and, as with their human counterparts, the peripheral damage is unacceptable. Trapping them simply makes the colony stronger and the only solution will be to control the water level. This will not get rid of them but it will protect the area from more damage. It is best done with a fenced siphon system.

That's where the challenge comes in. This is where beavers are at their best and earn their place as a symbol of Canadian identity: they are not afraid of hard work and they are resourceful, determined and not about to listen to reason.

Right now, though, it is January. It is snowing, it's getting a bit warmer outside and maybe a little too warm in Knotingham, the little log house that I have built to live in while I tackle the rest of the project.

CHAPTER 2

THE BUILDING TREE

WHAT MAKES A GOOD BUILDING TREE?

I am often asked what is the best kind of tree for building a log house. That is an easy question to answer because some trees are more resistant to decay, some have a better shape and some are more easily worked. The deciding factor is often which kind of tree is the most readily available and, in consequence, the cheapest to buy.

My reply to this question is that it is better to use good pine than bad Douglas fir, or good Douglas fir rather than bad cedar. However, if the materials are of an equally acceptable grade (the logs have a slow taper, are straight, sound and of a uniform size), then choose the logs on the basis of natural quality: resistance to decay, workability, strength and stability. A little explanation of these qualities is in order here.

Resistance to decay is the tree's natural ability to remain sound under adverse conditions. Cypress and cedar are at the head of this list, with larch and eastern hemlock not too far behind. But any tree will decompose quickly if conditions are favorable to decay. For best results, the logs should be protected from moisture, direct sunlight and infection from insects and bacteria.

Workability generally depends on how hard the wood is. Other factors to be considered are the nature of the grain of the wood, how many knots are to be found and if the form of the log is smooth or rough and irregular. Again cedar is at the top of the list, with spruce and pine close behind.

Strength is a different matter. Douglas fir is the strongest of western species. For most walls strength is not a problem, but for roofs it can be. This choice should be made according to how you're going to use the logs.

Stability refers to the reaction of the wood. If the grain (the direction in which the fibers lie) is straight and even, there is less tendency for the logs to move or twist. Some woods are more inclined to shrink and check (a condition caused by shrinkage that results in an erratic separation of the wood grain). This may

There are many techniques to make a crooked log fit.

at one time common and abundant. There are three reasons for this and the first and most important reason is agriculture.

At one time almost everyone was engaged in agriculture. There was little industry, particularly consumer-oriented industry, and no service sector as we know it today. Most people grew their own food, prepared it and preserved it where necessary. They provided their own entertainment and served their community as the need or occasion arose. But a population devoted to farming requires ever-increasing areas of land on which to grow crops and raise livestock. This means clearing the trees. Trees became the enemy: the major obstacle to wealth. This state of affairs prevailed into the 1940s and beyond, and with the coming of the bulldozer about that time, the trees lost the battle.

About the same time, expanding populations and economies provided growing markets for forest products. Trees became a consumer product, the second reason for their being in short supply.

Soon people no longer trusted a natural product and everything they wore, ate or lived in had to be subjected to some kind of processing before it was considered fit for human use. This brings us to the third reason why trees for your log house are not too easily found in the immediate neighborhood: technology. Technology was applied to the trees and they became just so many tons of fiber to be made into paper, chipboard, plywood, rayon and a hundred other things for the avid consumer to buy. We ate the trees around our cities like a groundhog clears the vegetation from the immediate vicinity of his burrow.

be related to moisture content and to the area of origin. Spruce and Douglas fir are inclined to shrink more.

AVAILABILITY

The question of what kind and size of tree to use will finally be settled by availability. The prospective builder must buy logs from a private source, or from commercial suppliers, domestic or foreign.

This brings up the interesting question of why logs are not available in those parts of the country, or indeed the world, where trees were

The Natural Tree

A natural tree is already a very good building material. It does not really need to be subjected to manufacturing processes and finishes. The cell structure of softwoods is somewhat like that of a honeycomb: tiny independent cells are sealed off from each other as the wood dries. This explains why the log, if left in its natural state with the cell structure undisturbed, has such an excellent insulating quality. The other part of the explanation of why solid timber has exceptional insulating qualities lies in what is called thermal mass: the tendency of a heavy object to heat or cool more slowly than a lighter object.

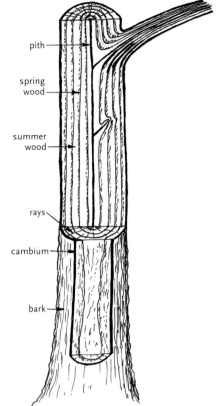

pith
spring wood
summer wood
rays
cambium
bark

The structure of softwoods.

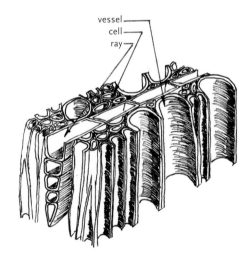

vessel
cell
ray

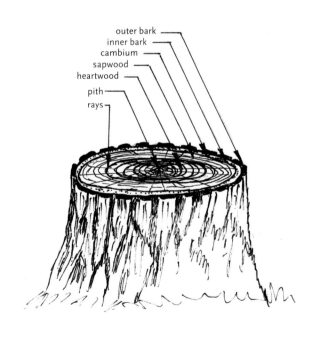

outer bark
inner bark
cambium
sapwood
heartwood
pith
rays

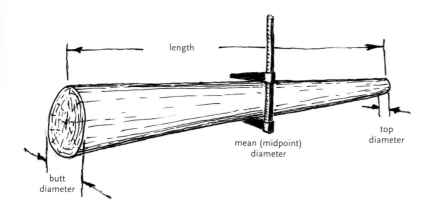

Log measurement. The average mean diameter is the most important consideration.

BUYING WOOD

Because it is now almost inevitable that you will buy your tree supply, you will have to negotiate with the supplier and specify the kind and size of the wood. Buy the best material that you can obtain. Extra money spent here will pay off many-fold in time saved and in the quality of the building. Spend extra to make sure that you get trees of a good size with butt ends that are not too flared. They should have a round shape to the trunk without too many knots or mechanically caused defects. The trees also need to have a small taper that ends in a good top size.

You will need to pay attention to the midpoint diameter of the log, because you want your walls to be of the same height, whether they are long walls or short walls. This is not, however, a common way to specify the purchase of logs, so you will have to specify length and top size and vary the lengths with the objective of cutting the logs to make up short pieces of the right diameter. For example, if you have a 2-m wall and a 6-m wall (including overhang), you might order 8-m logs and alternate using the large ends for the short wall and the long wall, to obtain an average height.

The logs may be purchased by the piece, by the load, by the ton or, most commonly, by the

Similar mean diameters are necessary so that long and short walls will reach the same height at the same time.

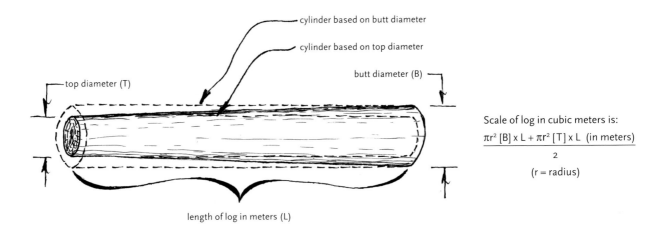

cylinder based on butt diameter

cylinder based on top diameter

top diameter (T)

butt diameter (B)

Scale of log in cubic meters is:

$$\frac{\pi r^2 \, [B] \times L + \pi r^2 \, [T] \times L \text{ (in meters)}}{2}$$

(r = radius)

length of log in meters (L)

cubic meter measurement. As a guide, one ton of wood in a partly dried state is very approximately one cubic meter. A Douglas fir log 12 m long with a 255-mm top will weigh one-half to three-quarters of a ton, or would be one-and-a-half to two logs per cubic meter. To determine the cubic meter measurement of the logs you are buying, see the table in the Appendix.

HARVESTING TREES

If you are among the most fortunate of people, you may have the opportunity to select and harvest your own trees from a private or public forest. This is an opportunity which should not be missed. It is a part of the whole experience. For an amateur, the work can be hard and extremely dangerous. This, in itself, is not sufficient reason to avoid the experience but rather a reason to learn the skill and take part in what is rapidly becoming a unique activity. It makes a lot more sense than bungee jumping. Harvesting trees is a productive challenge that provides the chance to do the job better and get the

right trees out with the least damage to the logs or the surrounding landscape. I will not attempt to cover all aspects of falling timber here: this job takes more skill, knowledge and dedication than is commonly understood. When you have finished, no one will be waiting to applaud. Only you will know, for the rest of your life, that you stood a little closer to the forest.

Your first job will be to thoroughly explore the vicinity in which you are to work. Walk the whole area and get to know the landscape and boundaries as well as the individual trees. As you begin to select trees, mark them with colored plastic ribbon or paint. Some trees may be a little smaller or larger than the size range you have decided on; they can be used for special purposes.

A good way to keep the size of trees within the limits you have set is to carry a piece of cord with two knots in it that represent the largest and smallest sizes you have selected. To measure the tree, place the cord around the circumference of the tree at a convenient height. Remember that the bark can make a big difference to the size of the log, so knot your cord with this in mind.

To determine where to put the knots on your cord, you must figure out the circumference of the size of trees you are looking for. Use the formula π x D, where π is pi (3.1416), and D is diameter. For example, if you are looking for trees that will measure 30 to 40 cm in diameter at breast height, you may determine that the bark is 2.5 cm in thickness on that size of tree. This will make the diameters 35 to 45 cm. Using the formula, your calculations will look like this:

3.1416 (π) x 35 (D) = 110
3.1416 (π) x 45 (D) = 141

Make your knots at 110 and 141 cm. (See Appendix for example using inches.)

Check the tree for form and height. Most trees in an older stand will be of a similar form. They may be fat, medium or thin (paraboloid, conical or nebraloid) in shape. Try to avoid the skinny trees. To check for straightness, stand back a short distance and look at the tree from two locations at right angles to each other. Most trees are straight from one side, but any sweep or crook will show from the other viewpoint.

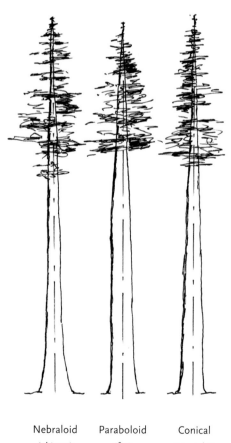

Nebraloid   Paraboloid   Conical
(skinny)   (fat)   (straight)

Trees that appear straight from one side may be quite different when viewed from another angle.

Felling a Tree

If the tree passes all tests, decide in which direction you want it to fall. Several factors enter into this decision: the lean of the tree, the wind direction, the slope of the land, the weight of the limbs or foliage, the surrounding trees, your escape path and the direction of removal. It is best to fell a tree into the direction that it leans, but if other considerations are important, the tree may easily be felled 90 degrees on either side of this or, with difficulty, in almost any other direction. If the slope of the ground is severe, it is best not to fell straight downhill because the tree reaches a great speed falling through the increased arc and may shatter or go on down the hill like a runaway locomotive. Generally, fell sideways across the hill.

Limbs all on one side of the tree can often be more significant than the lean of the tree. Once in New Zealand I attempted to fall a tree away from a road over which its abundance of

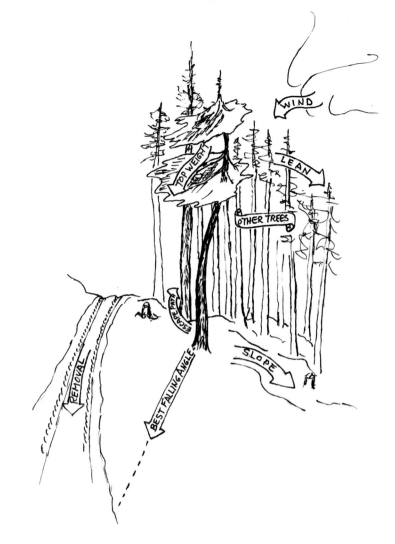

Basic Tree Felling

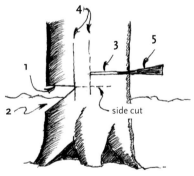

1 – Top of undercut. 2 – Humbolt undercut to save wood.
3 – Back cut. 4 – Retain more hinge wood on side away from lean. Make a side cut through sapwood if tree is falling into lean. Cut in from each side at a right angle to direction of fall to the depth of the sapwood. A leaning tree may fall too soon and the tough sapwood may tear out or split. The heartwood is more brittle and will break.
5 – Wedge should always be used.

1 – First cut: one-quarter to one-third of diameter. Cut must be level.
2 – Humbolt undercut (approved by Workers' Compensation) is used to minimize waste. It must meet first cut accurately. Minimum width: half the depth of first cut. 3 – Back cut: must be level and 25-50 mm above first cut. 4 – Hinge wood to control direction of fall. 5 – Wedge: place as soon as possible.

limbs were hanging. I tied a large rope 10 m up the tree and pulled this tight with a big farm tractor. I allowed the tractor to dig itself into the ground for extra holding power. The great macrocarpa tree fell across the road and took the tractor with it.

Try to fell the tree into the clear. If it is to brush against other trees it may hang or generate "widow-makers": limbs torn off trees as they brush past one another that are then thrown directly back at the feller. It may damage the other trees or lodge in tightly and become difficult to remove. Choose the path for removal and fell the trees in a herringbone (zigzag) pattern to, or away from, that path.

A branch (known as a "widow-maker") may be torn from falling tree and thrown directly back at you. Do not turn your back to a falling tree.

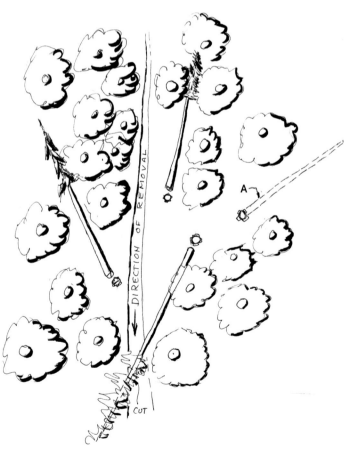

Ideal falling pattern for damage-free removal. Selective horse logging can be the best way to protect the stand with the least damage to the environment and leave the remaining trees in good condition. Fall herringbone to or away from the skid trail. Increase the angle to the trail for trees farther away (A).

Horse Logging

I am opposed to large-scale industrial exploitation of the forest. This is done with the primary purpose of producing immediate profits with little regard for the land, the trees, the environment or the future. The threat of lost jobs if we were to limit this practice does not have much credibility when you consider the many jobs that are being lost because of forest depletion.

I have done a lot of logging in my life. In the last fifty years I have worked in almost every job associated with the forest, from forest ranger to timber feller. The work that gave me the most pleasure was taking care of my own small patch of forest. To say that all misuse of the forest would be eliminated if it were in the hands of timber farmers is unrealistic, but it would be a step in the right direction.

Another step in the right direction would be to encourage horse logging. This method of extraction, coupled with good forest practice, is probably the most environmentally kind way to remove timber. I have worked with horses in steep country, deep snow and big timber. All the stories are true that tell of the patient, intelligent animals that become part of the crew. The horses will work almost on their own once they know their job. They know their rights and will stop work at exactly twelve noon and again at 4:30 p.m. They look forward to their meals with the same vigor as the rest of the camp. Complaints are rare. More importantly, horses do not dig up and destroy the earth and for them to work effectively, the felling and all the operation has to be done with skill. Now that most of the old growth timber has been removed from British Columbia,

horses are slowly returning to smaller, private operations on Vancouver Island and on the mainland. Perhaps this second time around, we will do a better job.

The Tree in Danger

People who build with logs come into direct contact with the natural material and soon come to understand the value of trees as part of their lives. While today almost everyone has become aware of the multitude of threats to forests and the forest environment, the world is under no immediate threat of extinction (at least from that direction). If we turn Central and South America and Malaysia into deserts to rival the sands of North Africa, we will not destroy the world, although we may destroy ourselves. The world has undergone catastrophic changes before and survived, changes that were the result of massive volcanic eruption, plate shift and asteroid impact.

Because we owe so much to the patient trees for our rise to dominance on the landscape, I feel that our continued well being is directly and predominantly associated with the trees. If we continue to decimate the flora and fauna of the planet at the present rate, we will destroy ourselves. As the tree is an endangered species, so are we.

The log builder is in the enviable position of being able to preserve a part of an endangered species. There are three methods of forest conservation that are of special concern to those who build with logs. Under the broad general aim of making optimum use of timber resources, he should be particularly aware of how he logs, how he builds and what he builds.

I advocate selective logging. This provides the opportunity to leave an undisturbed forest that will be able, within a few years, to provide its next crop. While I recognize the tendency in selective logging to remove the best and most profitable material first, this need not be the case. It has been demonstrated many times that good management in selective logging can result in stand improvement.

Any privilege, to endure, must be based in social responsibility. Therefore, how he builds is of special concern. If the ancient and honored craft is to survive he'll shape and fit logs as tightly as ships' timbers were fitted. His artistic judgment will put fine logs to their finest use, as did the 17th-century carpenters of Europe and Asia. He'll meet or exceed every aspect of national building codes. Let the log builder view this standard of work as straight economic dollars and sense. Or let

him build beautifully as an act of faith in the future, or a homage to the past. Whatever his motivation, the front-rank log builder knows that the road to excellence is the only way to go if we are to safeguard this great privilege of building with logs.

Therefore, what he builds can be safely assumed to be nothing except strong, handsome log buildings, well designed, well built, properly located and honestly achieved. But let me tell you that this assumption was hard to establish. Not long ago, a log building meant a hastily constructed "log cabin" with a dirt floor and leaky walls: something that would do while a "real" house was built. That image has now changed to one of a solidly built, beautiful and unique dwelling house. This represents a most significant milestone in the developmental sequence of the modern log-building renaissance.

Chapter 3

Planning

Early History of the Log House

Anywhere in the world, if there was a need for shelter, people made use of the available materials and tools to fill that need. We can therefore conclude that wherever trees were found and a permanent location and strong walls were desirable, some style of log building was invented. How these log houses were built and what style was adopted depended on location, climate, the kind of tools and timber available and the needs of the builders, as well as the social and political climate.

The earliest building (as opposed to caves that occurred naturally) seems to have been the pit house. Pit houses in central British Columbia were winter dwellings with access generally at the center pole. This style of shelter has found little following in today's world but still there is something to be learned from it, and what is now termed "underground housing" has reached a limited popularity in some parts of North America.

Log and timber-framed buildings originated

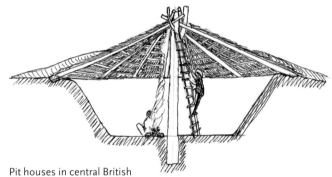

Pit houses in central British Columbia were winter dwellings and access was generally at the center.

Pole frame huts have been found worldwide.

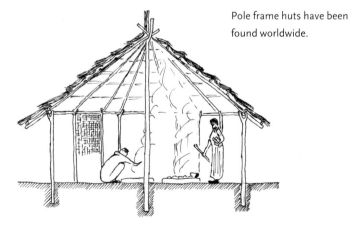

From a drawing by C.H.B. Quennell

in Africa and spread into eastern Europe, China and Japan, western and northern Europe and finally into North America, in much the same pattern as the migration pattern of populations.

In northern climates horizontal logwork developed, well fitted and often massive in proportion. The open post-and-beam style, finely decorated, evolved in the more southern climates.

Heavy post-and-beam or timber-frame construction has evolved for two reasons. First, it allows greater scope because design is not limited to the length of a tree. Second, it uses fewer trees, which can be necessary either because of financial concerns or the dwindling supply of suitable materials.

Both horizontal log construction and timber-frame construction reached a high degree of development in quality and design before the intrusion of manufactured building materials diverted attention to quicker and cheaper building systems.

It has been argued that the modern log building has gone a long way beyond any previous development in log buildings. This is true only in part. Although a modern log house may be technically or mechanically better, I believe that log houses in the past were superior from a spiritual or artistic point of view. Just what inspired this manifestation of spiritual awareness, whether it was a greater sensitivity to the forces of nature or whether they simply had more available time to devote to such contemplation, one can only speculate. What seems clear is that ancient builders had a far greater understanding of the nature of wood and how it would perform under different conditions, suggesting that their greater artistic ability arises from a more sensitive awareness of

and closer association with nature. In this regard we still have much to learn and, to me, this is the most interesting part of studying old buildings and old building methods.

The Log House in North America

Buildings always graphically display the development of the person or culture that built them. They cannot help but do so. We can read what our ancestors thought, dreamed or aspired to by looking at what they built. This will also be true for you and me. One day, others will look on what remains of our buildings and form conclusions about what we thought, what we dreamed and how much we cared.

With the influx of settlers from Europe into North America, a tremendous mixture of cultures and building traditions were thrown together. Over the two hundred years in which most of this migration took place, these different building customs encountered each other for the first time, often in an environment that was quite different from that in which they had been developed. As a result of this, in North America we inherited a wealth of building styles and design that otherwise might not have been available to us. People from Russia, Poland, England, France and northern Europe brought their axes of all different shapes and began to build with the trees that were found within hauling distance.

The French built grand houses in heavy timber and the Hudson's Bay Company built large and solid forts to protect their trading posts. A common form of log building for the workers or private settlers was a piquet or palisade house, adapted from the fortifications of native villages. They dug a trench the size and shape of the projected building and then erected a palisade wall around that perimeter. The earth was again compacted around these logs and the tops cut off in the shape of the roof. Some of these buildings still survive from the 17th century.

Many of the early buildings were poorly built by settlers who had little skill. However, there were some professional builders among them and good examples of solid timber buildings were scattered throughout the country. Hewn and dovetailed buildings are among the longest lasting and consequently we have many of these to study. The best were made of huge white pine trees and beautifully executed. Others were made of aspen and some of oak.

Round log buildings were of a more temporary nature, but some were well done and have survived. Of those that still serve their purpose, most have adequate foundations and good roof overhangs and are well located and scribe fitted. It is only in the last twenty years that round log buildings have come into their own. These new buildings are well designed, well built and make reverent use of the natural tree. So perhaps a new spiritual and artistic awareness is developing.

The size of the logs seems less important to longevity than design and roof protection, but the size of the logs makes a big difference to the appearance of the building. For my taste, I want to use the biggest logs that I can get. Short logs, however, can be very useful. Good design and skill can do much to make the best use of short logs and there are some advantages if you are thinking about building by hand.

Hewn-log house, Ontario, circa 1840. This house was built in Georgian style with white pine logs. Note that only six and seven logs were required to obtain the wall height.

Log size, design and the experience and the skill of the builder must all be considered if you are to build the best log house.

THE BEST LOG HOUSE

To build the best log house you must have a sheltered but ventilated site, protected from driving storms and intense sunlight but not so enclosed that it becomes mildewed and dank. Ideally this site would be on a slight rise of ground, more open on the north side, with trees to protect it from the prevailing storm winds and a roof overhang that would shield the walls from high summer sunlight. The foundation should be very strong and high. For most buildings, a foundation height of 200 mm above ground is considered adequate. For this house I think the foundation should be higher and even half a meter is not too much. The foundation should be stonework, or at least faced with stone, to give the building that connection to nature that we seek. There should be a good drip break at the bottom log and a

My first modern log home, the Kerry Street house in Prince George, British Columbia.

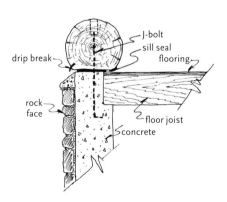

Foundation detail. A substantial foundation improves the life expectancy of any building and a stone facing helps give the house a strong connection to the earth.

drip break

rock face

J-bolt
sill seal
flooring

floor joist

concrete

moisture seal between the foundation and the first log because this is the most vulnerable place for decay and the intrusion of insects.

The logs should be of a good size: a minimum of 25 cm at the top for a family-sized house. They should be cut in winter and of a variety that is resistant to decay, such as cedar, cypress or Douglas fir. They should be peeled clean and treated with linseed oil (especially the ends), then fitted with skill and understanding. The roof should be designed carefully, for in the design of the roof lies the impact of the building. It should protect the house and control

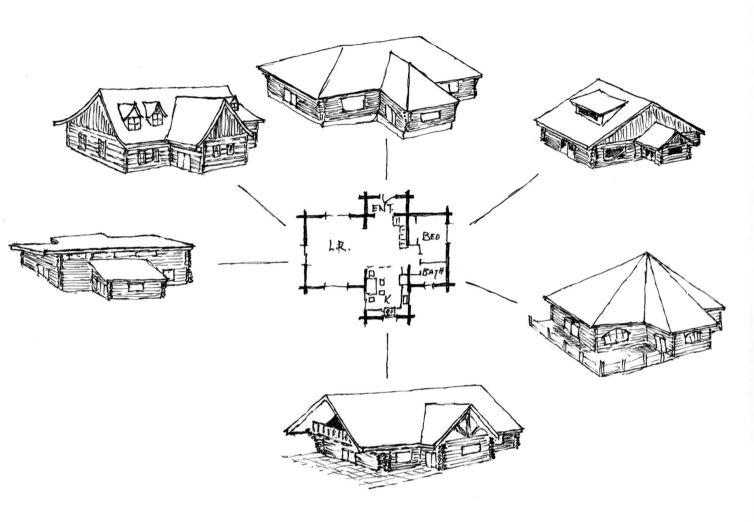

seasonal exposure to provide balanced light. Windows and doors should be handmade, or, if this is not possible, chosen with great care and they must be well fitted and the log-ends well finished. These six sketches illustrate that the same house plan can be designed many different ways.

Now, with the inclusion of amenities your work is well done. And the house must be lived in. Houses die if they are not lived in. They respond to laughter and joy and love and they last much longer. Now, you have built the best log house.

Site Selection

The site of our house is our real home. The house is just a convenient way to stay there. A building site may be chosen for all kinds of

These six sketches illustrate that the same house plan can be designed many different ways. Other variations would also be possible.

different reasons, particularly if it is for a second home. Some may wish to live high in the mountains while others want to be as deeply in the woods as is possible; some want to be near the ocean and others dream of a log house beside a lake. Each of these sites will have to be considered for its own sake in order to develop a harmony between you and the site. You will be considering the location with respect to the impact of the house on the site, the view, the light and the access.

There will be a reason why you chose this site in the first place. Is it the view? Is it the feeling of openness? Or seclusion? Is it because the site is close to the shopping center or did you just inherit it from your grandfather? The reason that you wish to build there should become central to your site plan and to your design. I recall one house built high up on a mountain slope, so high that it was difficult to get the logwork delivered. But it had a stupendous view overlooking a sweep of valley, several towns and on to the next mountain range. All this beauty was lost when the owner chose to place a blank wall and a bathroom facing the view, and set the large windows to look at the road. I never did find out why he did that.

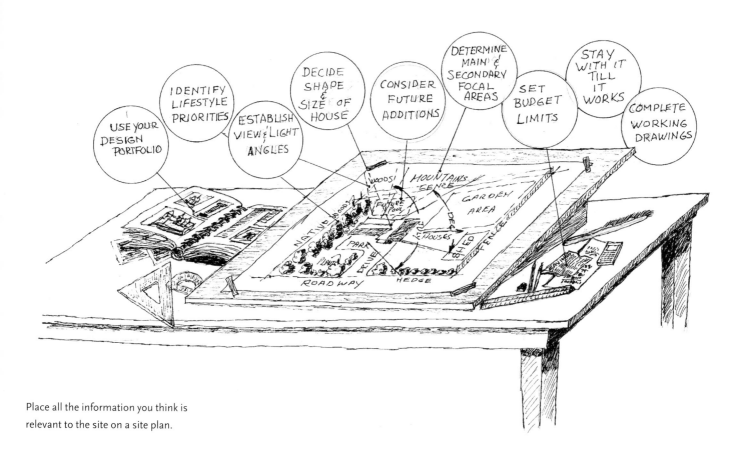

Place all the information you think is relevant to the site on a site plan.

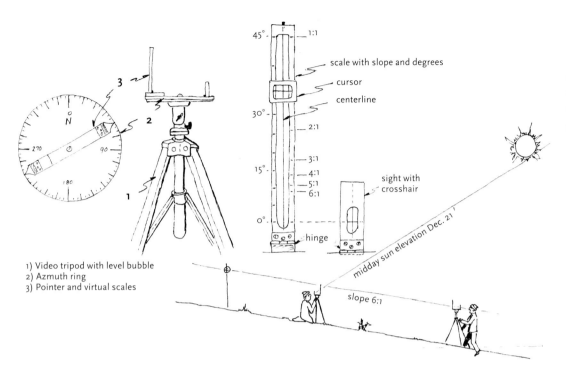

45° ——— 1:1

scale with slope and degrees

cursor

centerline

30° ——— 2:1

3 ——— 3:1
15° ——— 4:1
——— 5:1
——— 6:1

sight with crosshair

0° ———

hinge

midday sun elevation Dec. 21'

slope 6:1

1) Video tripod with level bubble
2) Azmuth ring
3) Pointer and virtual scales

A simple device made of plywood will serve to take site measurements for design purposes.

MAKING A SITE PLAN

For this reason it is important to see the site before plans are drawn. Make a site plan and locate the features that are important to you on this plan. This should be done with care and a fair degree of accuracy. If possible, plan this over the period of a year so that the change of season can be worked into the design. Visit the site until you get to know it. Sketch it. Feel it.

First, consider the impact of building on the site. If it is level, this consideration may only include the trees and vegetation to be found there, but if it is steep the impact can be very important. What kind of soil is there? Where does the water run in the wet season? Where do the trees get their water? If you level a building site here will it affect the stability of the site or the groundwater?

Next discover which views are important to you and draw them into the house location. Consider the vertical as well as the horizontal angles. Analyze the trajectory of the sun, particularly at midsummer and midwinter (June

Take time to evaluate a site. Get to know it in every mood and every season.

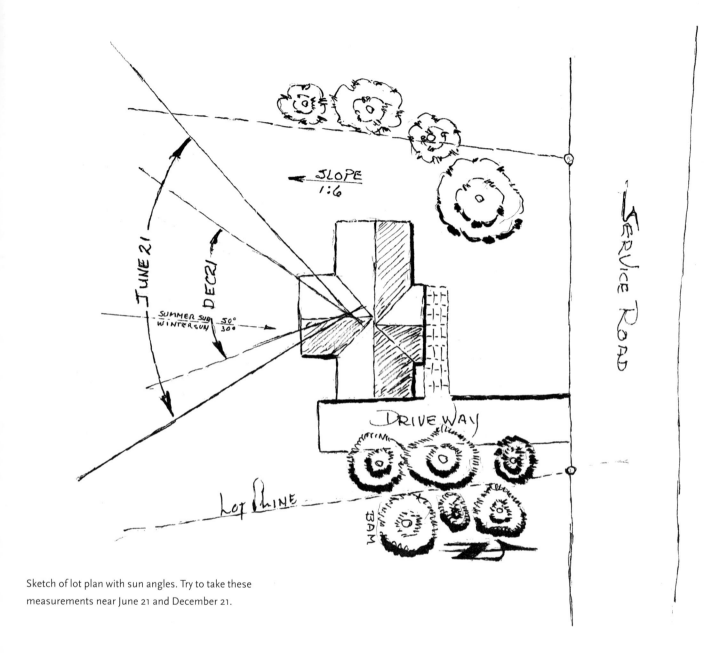

Sketch of lot plan with sun angles. Try to take these
measurements near June 21 and December 21.

21 and December 21) to see if your proposed
house location will get the best use of the sun.
This information is available on a computer
program for any location in the world, but it
might be more fun to generate the facts yourself. Place all this information on your site plan.
It can be used to determine the size and loca-

tion of windows, the placement of living areas
and the roof structure, especially the roof overhang, which will shade the walls and windows
in the summer and provide heat in the winter.

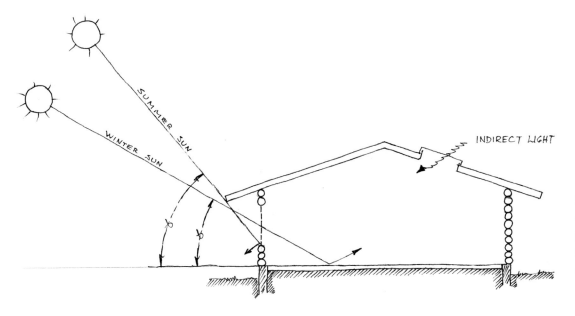

INDIRECT LIGHT

SUMMER SUN

WINTER SUN

Side elevation of house with sun path. This information will help with planning and design.

LIGHT

Of all the things that affect the overall feeling of a building, light and shadow are among the most important. Questions similar to the ones you asked about the sun and the views should also be asked about light. This is not necessarily the same thing as direct sunlight. You can have indirect or reflected light. This kind of light contains much less heat.

Which rooms do you want the strongest light in and at what times of the day? Research has shown that everyone has their own comfort mixture of both light and shade and you need to discover yours. This is how you do it. Imagine you are walking through a forest towards a large open meadow. As you start, the trees are very close together so that you can hardly see your way. But as you keep walking, the trees start to thin out and you can see the meadow in the distance. There will come a time when the mixture of light and shade feels exactly right for you. It may be deep in the forest or it may be out in the meadow.

On a suburban lot there is rarely any choice as to where to locate your house and it may seem useless to talk about improving the use of the sunlight or the view. Tight setback restrictions and the need to maximize any possible space usually means you will be building up to the limits available. The challenge is to get what you want in a confined space. But sun and light can be admitted through well-placed windows, skylights and light wells. It can be bounced off ceilings or sloped reflective surfaces. If you are planning a one-and-a-half-storey building with living space above, plan the view also from that height, where a whole different world may come into view.

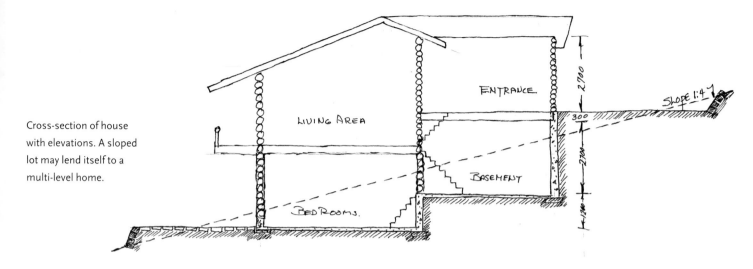

Cross-section of house with elevations. A sloped lot may lend itself to a multi-level home.

PLACEMENT OF THE HOUSE

If the lot has a definite slope you should make a scale drawing of the average slope. If the slope is greater than 1:4 (i.e., a drop of one meter in a run of four meters), then you should consider a split-level house with a lot of blank wall at the rear of the lower floor. If the lot is steeper, say 1:1, then you might plan the entrance to be onto the upper floor, with bedrooms on the lower floor. Sloping lots require more imagination but they also provide a greater opportunity to build an interesting structure. Think of the house as a collection of living spaces rather than a single platform, and then create interconnected links.

A sloped site, however, requires more attention to structural planning to make sure that the foundations are adequate and the slope is stable. One other thing in a split-level log house is the differential in wall settlement. In other words, the higher wall will settle more than the lower wall, because it contains a greater height (and weight) of wood. While this

is not a problem to an experienced builder, the first-time builder is cautioned to consider this with care. A large development lot of a half hectare or more provides room for the designer to work without having the worry of providing access and services. But the choice of a proposed building site is fairly limited within a property this size, so survey work can be kept to a minimum.

Finding the best building site on a large acreage may take more time and imagination. But then the reward is greater too: the building may now fit more comfortably within the site, the desired view and exposure can be obtained and site impact may be kept to a minimum.

With a larger rural property, the builder is confronted with space and the need to make serious decisions as to where to locate the house. Often the decision is to place the house right next to the road, the same way as in the city. This gives top priority to access and convenience and, indeed, in some cases this may still be the best location. In northern climates where deep snow is involved, easy access can be a serious consideration. This has never been a deterrent to me, however, and when we built any of our own houses, we put them where we wanted them and solved the problems of access on their own merit. While I still retain sharp memories of sitting on an unbelievably cold snowplow throughout the night in order to get the kids to school the next day, I include these experiences in my list of fond memories because I was providing for my own needs in an independent way.

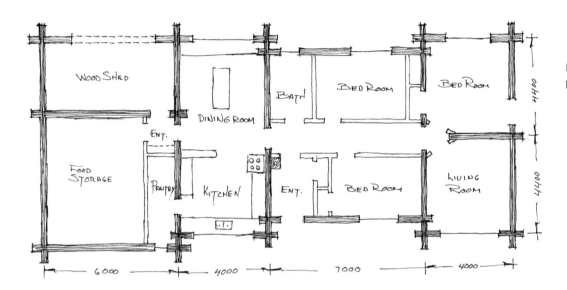

Floor plan of ranch house at Silloep Hills.

The ranch house at Silloep Hills was three kilometers off the road. Access was always exciting, but the view was well worth the minor difficulty of snowplowing.

CHAPTER 4

MAKING A SET OF PLANS

GETTING ORGANIZED

By this time you have reached the point where you are determined to build a log house. You know why you want to build with logs and you know the historical background for your undertaking. You know how you intend to accomplish all this and you know what to look for in your site plan.

Now all you need is time, money and a plan on paper.

All three of these will have to be considered together. How long it will take to build and how much it will cost are related directly to the house plan. The plan will be affected by considerations of lifestyle, traffic patterns, site, location and personal design priorities.

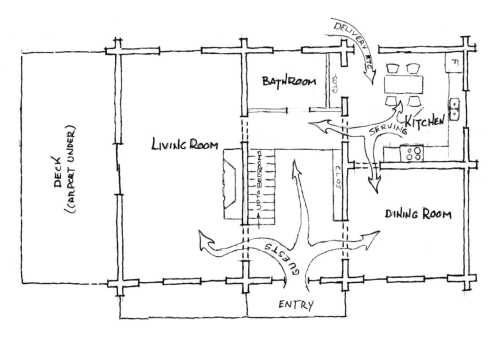

Kerry Street house with traffic pattern. Traffic lines may meet and merge but not cross. This pattern might be expected in the evening.

Preliminary sketches will establish scale and important relationships. This plan meets budget, lifestyle, site location and ability.

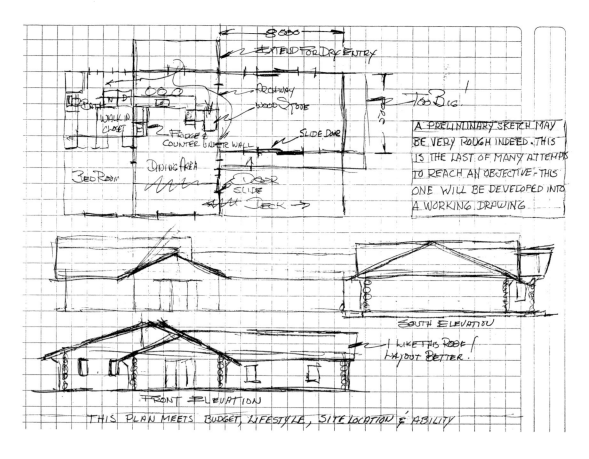

In all of this exercise, I am going to presume that you will be doing this whole project yourself. This is the best way to get the full benefit of the experience: since this is most likely a once-in-a-lifetime undertaking, working out exactly what it is you want in your building is your job and you should do it all by yourself. This is not to say that you are not able to seek advice or opinion from others, but the final decisions should be your own.

Now, whether you are an experienced builder or not, you will be going through a well-established series of steps to bring your dream into reality. These steps are:

1) Work out exactly what you want to build in a set of preliminary drawings and sketches.

This should take into account budget, lifestyle, site and ability.

2) Produce a set of detailed drawings.

3) Obtain permits and authorizations as required, both local and regional. Check surveys, utilities and access.

4) Invite bids and quotes from contractors or suppliers for the portion of the building that will be contracted out.

5) Work out a plan of operation. This may be a general plan or you may wish to go to the extent of making a detailed flow chart.

Design Portfolio

A simple house might be built with very little on paper. However, this is not necessary – nor is it a good idea. Most municipal authorities will want to see a reasonable set of plans before issuing permits. So take a little time and make a set of plans, even if you are not very good at this sort of thing and you know little or noth-

ing about drafting. You can learn, and in the process of drawing you will probably discover a lot about the house you wish to build, and maybe make it a better one as well.

You can hire an architect or an architectural designer to do this work. They are usually very competent and able to handle any complexities that arise. However, an architect's fee may be ten percent of the final building cost, and

FRONT ELEVATION Nº1

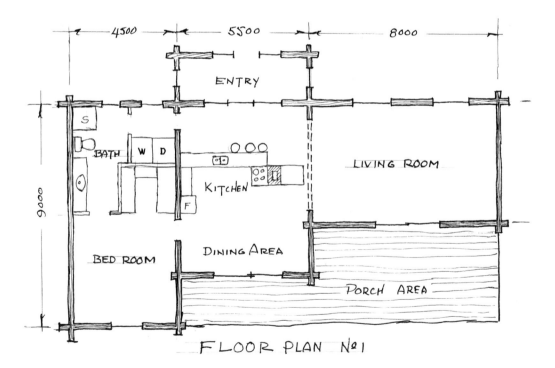

FLOOR PLAN Nº1

A simple house may need only minimal drawings: a floor plan and one elevation.

FRONT ELEVATION №2

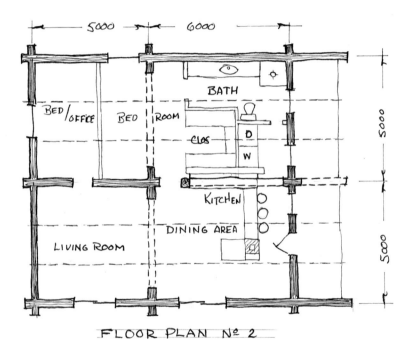

FLOOR PLAN №2

Plan for a small house. This information can be further developed as required.

though an architectural designer's fee may be less, most will want to include their own creative input, and this may be contrary to your original ambition.

If you are going to do this project right from the start, now is a good time to begin. You will need a set of building codes and standards, particularly the sections dealing with log buildings. You will need some drafting equipment and about one hundred hours of available time.

Start by putting together a design portfolio. This can be a loose-page binder that you can use to organize all the photos, magazine clippings and sketches you have been saving for the last several years. You should include as many aspects of the building as you can: rooflines, window treatment, doors and furniture, as well as floor layouts and elevations. Your final design is to be what you want and there is no better way to find out than to collect examples of what strikes you as good and organize them for reference. Don't worry about costs or practical applications at this time; you are only establishing the effect that you want. How you are to achieve this is a different matter – the important thing at this point is not to compromise. Get a good sketch book (228 x 300 mm is a good size) and save all your sketches. Even after the project has been completed, these will be an ever-increasing source of pleasure to you.

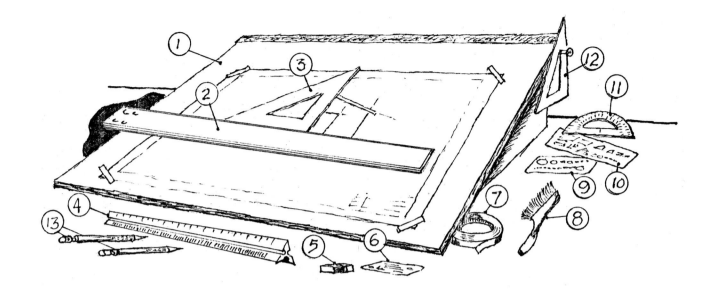

BASIC AND LOW-COST DRAFTING EQUIPMENT

1) Drawing board – 750 x 1000 mm minimum, larger if you have space. Green vinyl cover, tape to top only.
2) T-square – should be almost length of board
3) 45° plastic square – not too big, about 250–350 mm per side
4) Scale rule – or just a good metric rule
5) Eraser – get the best you can find
6) Eraser shield – very handy
7) Masking tape – 12 mm wide
8) Brush – a light one to clear eraser dust
9) Hole template
10) Architectural template – 1:50 and 1:100 scales
11) Protractor – get a good big one
12) 30°/60° triangle – all templates can hang on hook
13) Mechanical pencils – .3 or .5 mm – suitable hardness

DRAFTING EQUIPMENT

Drawing can be done on the kitchen table with a pencil, straight-edge ruler and graph paper, but basic drafting equipment is not expensive and you would be well advised to obtain a functional set. This would consist of a board (which could be made of plywood with a vinyl cover) at least 750 x 1000 mm, a T-square and a set square (preferably one that locks onto the T-square).

In addition, you will want a scale rule and two mechanical pencils: one .3 mm and one .5 mm, with leads of a hardness suitable to the drawing medium you plan to use (for velum use HB and for mylar use H or 2H) and a good eraser. From here the sky is the only limit and you can get as much or as complex a set of tools as you wish. But if you are going to do only the one plan, the money may be better spent on tools to build the house.

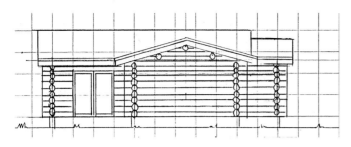

North Elevation 1:200

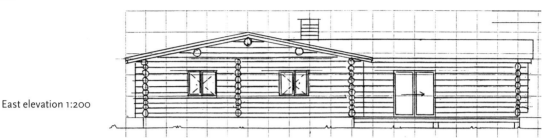

East elevation 1:200

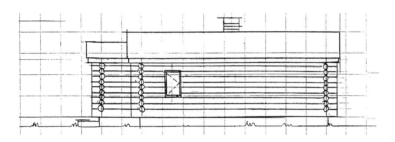

South elevation 1:200

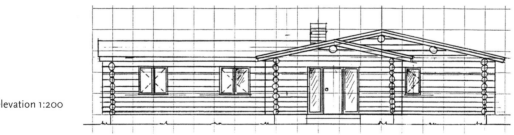

West elevation 1:200

BASIC PLANS AND ELEVATIONS

You do not need to be an artist to draw basic plans and elevations. There are just three basic views for a residential dwelling: plans, elevations and cross-sections.

Along with the plans and elevations, you may wish to illustrate some details of just how everything is to go together. A set of plans is a means of communicating your ideas to others with both pictures and explanations. Study other plans to see how this is done (see my book, *Log House Plans).*

Your original plans will be single-line

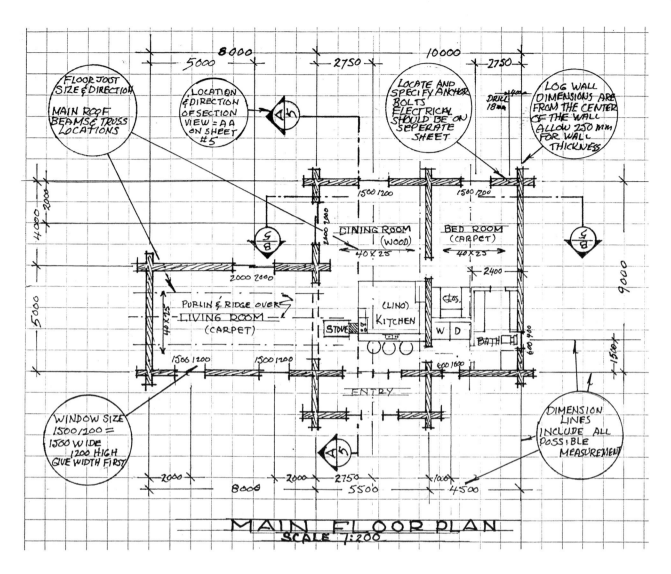

Floor plan with the elements that might be included.

drawings, which do not allow for wall thickness. In your more formal floor plans, done with double lines, be sure to allow 300 mm for the average wall and a minimum of 1 m by 3 m for stairs. Choose an appropriate location on your sheet of paper to place your first formal plan, since you will be using this paper for several drawings. Choose a suitable scale. Drawing to scale is an important part of the job and provides you with proportions and perspectives on your lifestyle.

COMMON SCALES

Site plans	1:200
Plans and elevations	1:100 or 1:50
Working drawings	1:50
Details	1:25 or 1:12

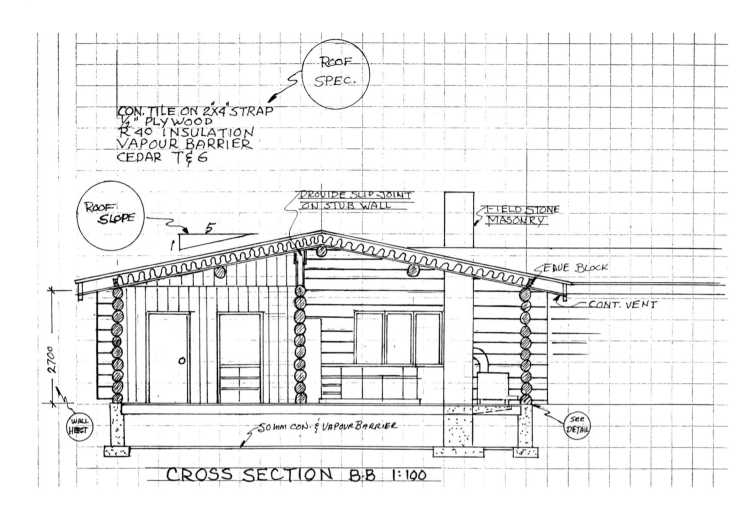

ROOF
SPEC.

CON. TILE ON 2×4" STRAP
½" PLYWOOD
R 40 INSULATION
VAPOUR BARRIER
CEDAR T & G

ROOF
SLOPE

PROVIDE SLIP JOINT
ON STUB WALL

FIELD STONE
MASONRY

EAVE BLOCK

CONT. VENT

2700

WALL
HEIGT

50 mm CON. & VAPOUR BARRIER

SEE
DETAIL

CROSS SECTION B·B 1:100

Cross-section with expected elements noted.

For log buildings I use a standard wall thickness of 300 mm and dimension everything from the centerline of the wall. This means that I write in the length of the actual measurement so the builder can work from accurate measurements and not have to convert from scale. Measuring from the centerline is not usual in building plans, but if you consider it for a while you will realize that this is the only stable measurement possible in a wall of tapered and often crooked logs. Framed walls may be shown as 150 mm wide while foundations would be a minimum of 200 mm and footings a minimum of 400 mm.

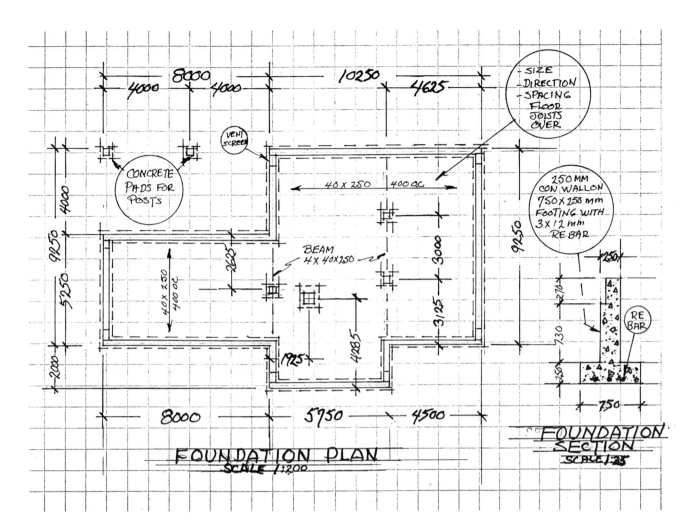

Foundation plan.

From the floor plan you can develop the foundation plan and the elevations. I find it useful to work on all of these at the same time so that I don't go ahead too far on any one aspect in case a problem shows up that requires alterations to any of the drawings.

Site plan for Shanty Lake.

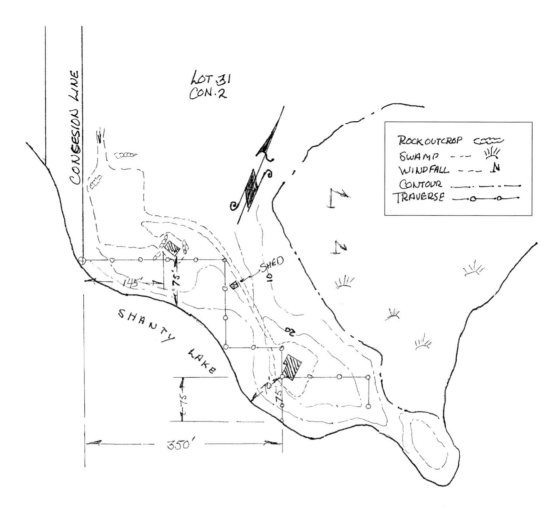

PLANNING YOUR ENVIRONMENT

In your house plan, also plan for the environment, in the house and as far out beyond the house as it is possible for you to do so. Even if you own only a very small lot, it is possible to create a personal environment inside the house and to surround the living space with a compatible design. Of course, everyone has a different style of living and it would be impossible for me to anticipate what any individual preference might be. I have had the impression in the last few years that log buildings have come to imitate suburban framed-house design. This kind of building is too often popular because of its functional efficiency. I have no objection to functional efficiency unless quality of living has to be sacrificed, but too often this is exactly the case as we are led farther and farther away from our ancestral roots. Many city dwellings are extremely efficient but even the most ingenious decorator will, in my opinion, be hard put to make it into a warm and comfortable home.

*Evaluating the Shanty Lake site
the first winter.*

I found this property in October, 1998. The purchase was finalized in December of that year but I was not able to start until March, 1999. I decided to take my own advice and build a guest house of logs to live in while building the main house to avoid rushing the construction of the main house.

The logs would have to be cut in the winter and delivered before spring for two reasons: spring-cut wood is vastly inferior and because there was no road, the spring mud made it impossible to transport anything heavy. In the process of obtaining logs for the project I discovered a wonderful person and friend – Mr. Paul Pitkanen. Paul was a log builder working in the general area and he let me use his building site to pre-build my small house. This enabled me to start work much sooner than I would otherwise be able to do. Paul also knew where there were a set of building logs that the owner wanted to sell. I did not look at these logs. I tried to, but they

Plans for the guest house at Shanty Lake (facing and following pages). Knotingham (the name is intended to describe the appearance of the logs) was built, to some extent, the old way. That was a bit of self-indulgence because after years of working in association with the building industry and its rigidity, I needed to do something more casual and build in a more relaxed way. I used only the simple tools, although I did use a chainsaw. In order to be as fully relaxed as possible, I dispensed with transit levels, saw guides and metric measurements. As someone said, "To walk 1.6 km in the other fellow's moccasins just doesn't have the same poetry."

were under a meter of snow. But there was a lump in the snow at the designated location so I bought this lump for $2400. There were supposed to be thirty-two peeled 9-m logs.

I bought a backhoe at an auction and moved it up to Paul's site, located a self-loading truck and dug out my set of building logs. There were twenty-eight logs and, indeed, a few of them were 9 m long. The logs were eastern hemlock: short, tapered and bristling with knots. Did I mention that they were not too straight? The wood itself was a good choice. Eastern hemlock is a far more resistant wood than western hemlock and not quite as hard. Paul thought that there would be enough logs to build a house about 4 x 5 meters. In my years of teaching log building around the world I have encountered a wide variety of materials and a wide spectrum of quality and form, and I have also acquired a certain amount of experience. I decided to make the building 5 x 7 meters.

By this time most of the planning was in place. I had made plans for the little house and the main house. I had maps and air photos as well as on-site experience of the proposed location. The site was to be on the north side of the lake. The shoreline is ringed with birch and over-mature poplar. The land is solid rock outcrop and piles of boulders mixed with clay and swamp, which is probably one of the more difficult types of terrain for road building. Fortunately there is no permafrost.

Ultimately I expect to have a house; a shed for machinery, tools and a workshop; woodsheds (of course); a sauna and guest houses for my friends. Knotingham will become the first guest house when I am finished with it (if, by then, I still have any friends).

There were several options open for the material I had to build with. A pit house would be quick and easy with a backhoe to do the work, but the type of soil on the site would soon have made it into an indoor pool. We considered a wall tent: that would be quick. I did plans for a frame building but somehow it looked too out of place. A post-and-beam building would certainly be a valid choice. Transporting the materials into the site might be a little easier than for a solid log house, and the cost would be about the same. A post-and-beam structure, much like timber frame, is more of a skeleton of logs with panels between the posts. Plywood and wallboard would be the logical choice to complete the panels, but I prefer solid timber, and this is part of the reason for choosing logs.

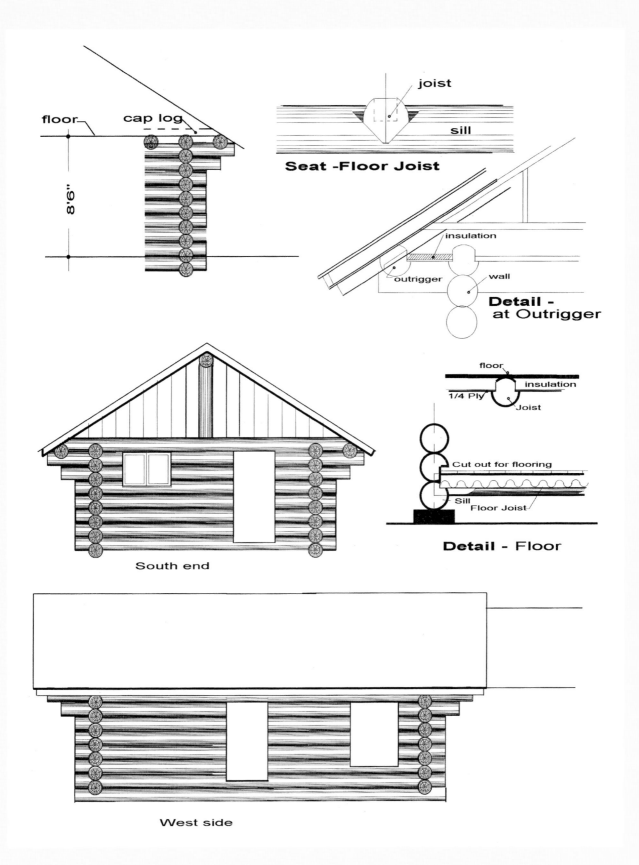

floor

cap log

8'6"

joist

sill

Seat -Floor Joist

insulation

outrigger

wall

Detail - at Outrigger

floor

insulation

1/4 Ply

Joist

Cut out for flooring

Sill

Floor Joist

Detail - Floor

South end

West side

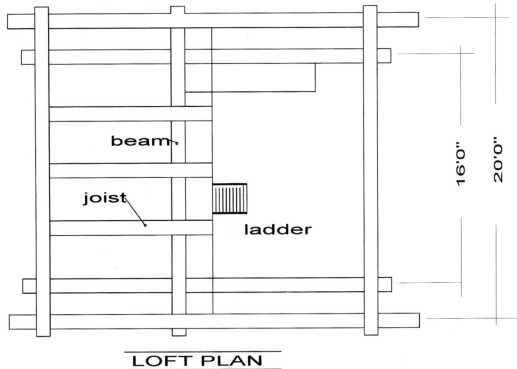

beam

joist

ladder

16'0"

20'0"

LOFT PLAN

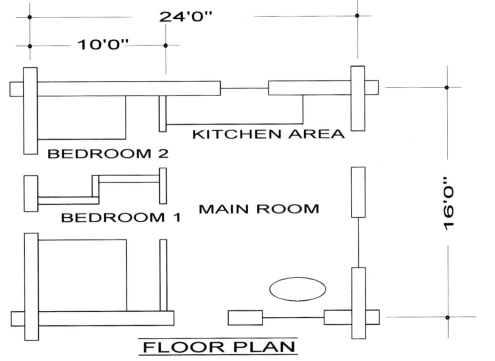

24'0"

10'0"

KITCHEN AREA

BEDROOM 2

BEDROOM 1   MAIN ROOM

16'0"

FLOOR PLAN

CHAPTER 5

HOW LONG WILL IT TAKE AND HOW MUCH WILL IT COST?

ESTIMATING BUILDING TIME

The first log house took several million years to build. Fortunately, we have improved this timetable considerably since those days. Nevertheless, if we realistically consider the time it takes to grow the trees that are used in the construction of the house and the time needed for nature to provide the site on which the house is built, it still takes a very long time to build a log house. However, once these preliminaries have been accomplished, the actual work involved in the undertaking can be completed within a reasonable time frame. Good planning, good organization and experience will serve you well.

First make an honest evaluation of the factors that will affect the length of the project. These will be:
- size and style of the building
- experience of the builder
- time available for work
- money, tools and equipment available
- prevailing weather conditions.

Before going ahead with the actual building, decide how you are going to handle each of these issues. These are considerations even if money is not a limiting factor.

The first log house took several million years to build.

Design considerations can have a dramatic effect on the cost of a project.

Assess your experience and your skills. If you feel you need instruction or practise, these services are available. I tell so many students that the time spent to take a course of instruction – even one week – will pay off in money saved, time saved and in the improved quality of the building produced. This holds true even for those buildings that are to be contracted out, because an informed owner will be much more able to manage the undertaking. Even consider taking a job with an experienced builder as an apprenticeship experience. The time spent will pay great dividends in the eventual building.

It is obvious that a large building is going to be more time consuming than a small building. What may not be quite so obvious is that the style of the building can have an impact on the length of time required to do the job. A fancy or elaborate design can add a surprising amount of time to the work schedule. This kind of design can also become tiresome in a few years, especially if it has not been done with care.

Look at the plan and design you have selected in this light and consider changing the overall size or reducing the number of corners or just simplifying the whole structure.

The time available to you for the required work can also be modified. If you plan to build as a weekend undertaking, you can organize equipment, tools and additional help to offset the limited hours available, plan the work at a time of year when there will not be too much weather damage and perhaps schedule holidays or time off in order to make the final important effort to get the roof on before the rainy season.

Site preparation and organization may be the first year's undertaking.

The Economical Approach: Do It Yourself

The time required to build and the cost of building are very closely related. There are, however, factors that are unique to log buildings that may require some additional explanation. Because the labor component of a log building is proportionately greater than that of a frame building, experience becomes more important in controlling costs. It is possible to build a log house with very little outlay of cash money if you have the imagination, ingenuity and experience to do the work yourself. And this is the kind of house that you are building: a house that is spiritually sound as well as technically sound. Such a house requires the greatest possible proportion of the work to be done by you.

I will assume that you have purchased the site for the house and it is just what you want. Otherwise this would be the time to make a change, before you have invested more time in it. Do all the site preparation first. This may become the first year's work. If you wish to proceed faster, do so, but do not shortcut this preliminary preparation work. Site preparation will include access; clearing as necessary; drainage and sewer; water, electrical and telephone access; foundation and rough landscaping.

Access, clearing, drainage, underground services and landscaping layout may well be undertaken by a machine. No one working by hand can compete with a backhoe when it comes to digging out stumps, trenching or just generally moving tons of material. But when it comes to working with care and the impact on the environment, the person who works by hand has a distinct advantage. Stumps can be

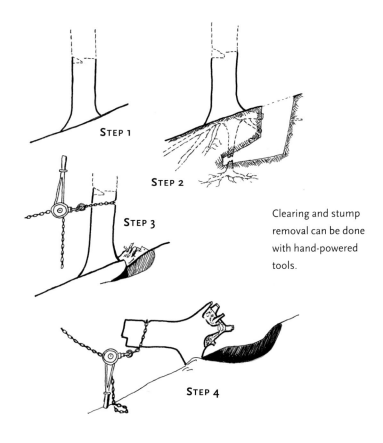

Clearing and stump removal can be done with hand-powered tools.

removed by hand and with surprising ease in many instances. A road, even a long one, can often be built by hand with less labor than it takes to clean up after a bulldozer. If a basement is not required (as in the house plan I have chosen), careful placement of the building can eliminate much of the work involved in preparing the location, while at the same time providing a more natural setting.

Plan 793.

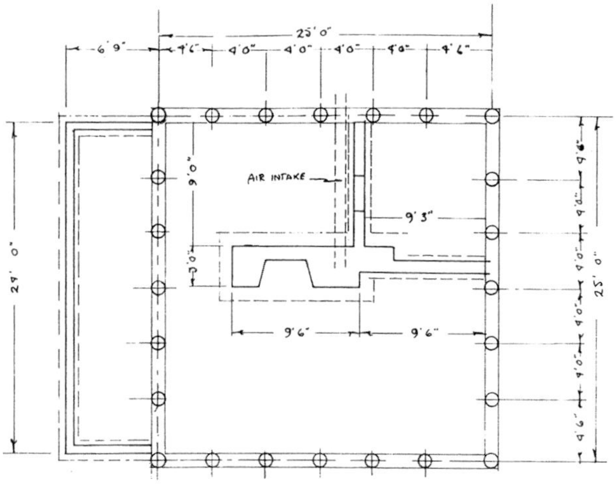

FOUNDATION PLAN
SCALE ¼" = 1'

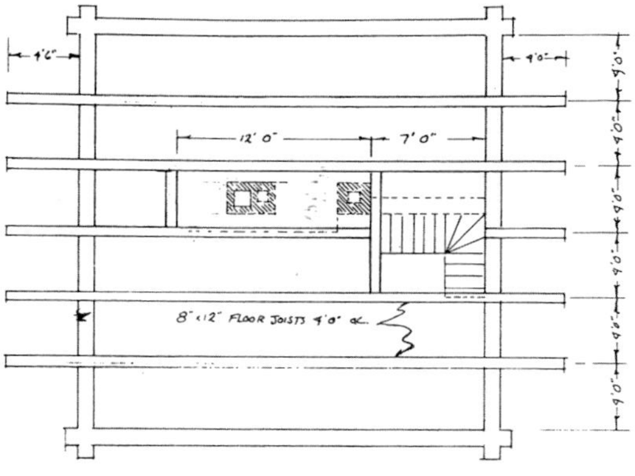

AIR INTAKE

DETAIL – SECOND FLOOR JOISTS

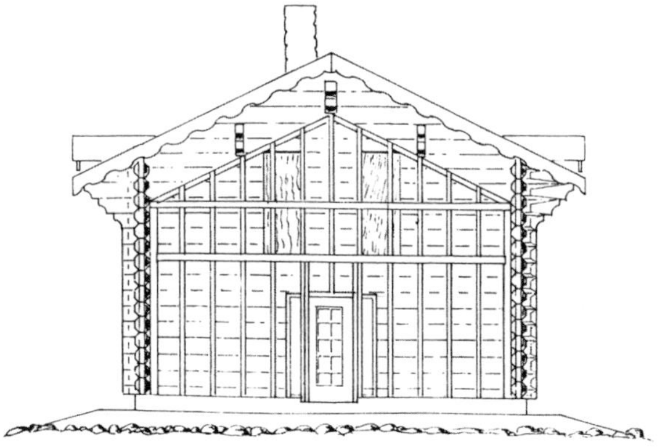

8"×12" FLOOR JOISTS 4'0" oc.

SOUTH ELEVATION

WEST ELEVATION

A Simple House

The plan I have chosen here is Plan 793 in the book *Log House Plans*. It is a design of which I am very fond and one which, in certain locations, would suit me very well. On a level site there would be little digging because the foundation is raised above the ground level and filled. Treated wood posts can be substituted for concrete posts and the minimal amount of concrete needed can then be placed by hand with the help of a rented or borrowed concrete mixer.

The walls are drawn as hewn logs, although that is a matter of taste. The main thing is that the walls are not long, only 8 meters, and the house is two storeys high to save on roof structure and heating. It is a small house. The fireplace is large to retain heat and houses the water system, making it less vulnerable to frost. The sauna and passive solar greenhouse are optional, but if you build them you will save water and power. This house is designed for a cold location but would work well almost anywhere. I could build this house all by hand and take great pleasure in doing so. Trenching for services may also be done by hand, but whether you hire a machine, hire a worker or do it all yourself is a decision you alone can make.

With this work done, the next consideration is the logwork. Most likely, for reasons which I have already pointed out, you will have to buy this material. The price of logs can vary a great deal but that cost is still a minor part of the overall budget. It is always cost-effective to use good logs because time and labor is thereby reduced.

Have the logs delivered as close to the house site as is practical so that you can use manual lifting devices to raise the logs from here to the top of the walls (see Chapter 6).

A PERSONAL ESTIMATE

A log house does not easily fall within the ordinary cost of production analysis because there are too many variables. Everything depends on how much of the material the builder is able to obtain at a low cost (such as logs, shakes, rock, lumber...), and how much of the labor the family is able to do themselves at little or no cost. Only the individual home owner can calculate what his expenses will be.

Whatever number you come up with, it is at best only an estimate. It may be useful to obtain an estimate sheet such as contractors use (see "Blueprint Estimate for a Log Shell, p.68) to list every conceivable item. It is only to be expected that the more you do or obtain for yourself, the lower the cost. At the other end of the scale, if everything is done by a contractor, the project can be expected to cost the maximum. This is not unreasonable, since you will be getting good value, but doing it yourself will save you money.

When estimating your costs, take the following factors into consideration.

1) Cost of material
This is the cost of the logs delivered to the work site. These may be logs cut to length and peeled or they may be full-length logs, sorted for size and unpeeled. The price will be for a cubic meter of wood and will have to be converted to a cost per lineal meter of log.

2) Labor
This includes peeling, placing, fitting, trim cuts, door and window cuts, roof-system construction, stairs and railings, sanding, preservative or other treatment, any special work and moving the completed work to the permanent site (loading out). Because you will be doing most of your own work, this only applies to the jobs you will be hiring out.

3) Equipment and supplies
This will include costs for cranes, machine rentals, chainsaws, power tools, hand tools, fuel and repairs. If you place the logs by hand and work with hand tools, this figure will be low.

4) Overhead
This is the cost of investment charges, rentals, blueprints, insurance, supervision, fees, permits and vehicles. Again, if you do the work yourself, this figure will be low.

Any formula or system of estimation will have to be adjusted as needed by your experience and changing conditions. No formula can be expected to function in all localities and under all building conditions. The completion of the house is considered separately from the construction of the shell because the shell may be built at a location removed from the actual building site. Transportation, re-erection and all the other aspects of the finished house should be detailed on the estimate.

THE BUTTERFLY EFFECT

How long does it take to build a log house? How much does it cost? These are questions that we will never be able to answer fully because we do not have a suitable means to measure these costs. Before we had access to these beautiful trees, this blue and green world (which we mistakenly take for granted) went through unimaginable eons of development. That this mass of molten rock ever became a haven for life, unique within our perception, is a matter for wonder. That it should become a complex set of interacting and self-stabilizing systems is a matter that more than challenges our best attempts at understanding.

It is becoming more and more obvious that our present attitudes and activities are tending to destabilize the comfortable environment we depend upon for our existence. We are not able to predict with any real assurance just what the results of our actions will be, but responsible scientists present scenarios that range from massive disruption to the total elimination of life as we now know it. The butterfly effect is the term used for the theory that postulates (tongue in cheek) that a butterfly flapping its wings in Colorado may initiate a hurricane in Malaysia. The world has a history of being able to survive catastrophic impact; the question is whether we, as a species, can.

I have always claimed that building with logs is not an attempt to return to a simple way of life from the past, but rather that it is a method of construction that does the least harm to the forest while we attempt to discover ways to eliminate destructive building practises. It is important that we fully understand what the results of our actions will be before we undertake any quick fix to the environment.

But I believe that we must make a concentrated effort: replant and reserve the rain forests; reduce and eliminate carbon dioxide emissions and restore the health of the oceans. If we do not find the ways to make these changes, the day will come when the next log house may again take several million years to build.

BLUEPRINT ESTIMATE FOR A LOG SHELL

Item	Cost	Item	Cost
MATERIAL		**EQUIPMENT AND SUPPLIES**	
Logs	_____	Machine rental	_____
Waste +10%	_____	Tools	_____
Labor	_____	Gas and oil	_____
Peel	_____	Site cleanup	_____
Groove	_____	Miscellaneous	_____
Notch	_____	*Equipment and Supplies Subtotal*	_____
Doors	_____		
Windows	_____		
Wall end	_____		
Trim	_____	**OVERHEAD**	
Sand	_____	Insurance	_____
Post	_____	Telephone	_____
Log-ends	_____	Hydro	_____
Electrical holes	_____	Wages	_____
Through-bolts	_____	Miscellaneous	_____
Floor cuts	_____	*Overhead Subtotal*	_____
Partition cuts	_____		
Plate cut	_____		
Upper floor cuts	_____	**TOTAL ESTIMATE**	_____
Temporary foundation	_____		
Stairs	_____		
Railings	_____		
Treatment	_____		
Load-out	_____		
Miscellaneous	_____		
Material Subtotal	_____		

Preliminary Costs Estimate

Item	Estimate	Quote	Totals
PLANS AND PERMITS			
Building permits	_____	_____	_____
Working plans	_____	_____	_____
Lot plan	_____	_____	_____
Percolation test*	_____	_____	_____
Survey fees	_____	_____	_____
Plans and Permits Subtotal			_____
SITE			
Clear site	_____	_____	_____
Soil test	_____	_____	_____
Entrance road	_____	_____	_____
Bridges	_____	_____	_____
Gate and fencing	_____	_____	_____
Site Subtotal			_____
INSURANCE			
Title insurance	_____	_____	_____
Public liability	_____	_____	_____
Builder's risk	_____	_____	_____
Workers' compensation	_____	_____	_____
Fire, theft, vandalism	_____	_____	_____
Vehicle and equipment	_____	_____	_____
Bonding	_____	_____	_____
Insurance Subtotal			_____
TOOLS AND EQUIPMENT			
Hand tools	_____	_____	_____
Chainsaws	_____	_____	_____
Power tools	_____	_____	_____
Log-moving equipment	_____	_____	_____
Log-lifting equipment	_____	_____	_____
Maintenance, tools and equipment	_____	_____	_____
Gas and oil	_____	_____	_____
Operating supplies	_____	_____	_____
Tools and Equipment Subtotal			_____

*a percolation test measures the rate water is absorbed into the soil

Item	Estimate	Quote	Totals
EXCAVATION			
Remove and stockpile topsoil	_____	_____	_____
Cut, fill and grade	_____	_____	_____
Basement	_____	_____	_____
Septic tank	_____	_____	_____
Septic field	_____	_____	_____
Swimming pool	_____	_____	_____
Sewer	_____	_____	_____
Telephone and television	_____	_____	_____
Water	_____	_____	_____
Heat (propane, gas, oil)	_____	_____	_____
Electrical	_____	_____	_____
Cablevision	_____	_____	_____
Water line and fees	_____	_____	_____
Sewer line and fees	_____	_____	_____
Water well and permits	_____	_____	_____
Septic system and permits	_____	_____	_____
Excavation Subtotal			_____
FOUNDATION			
Concrete and footings	_____	_____	_____
Pier pads*	_____	_____	_____
Foundation walls	_____	_____	_____
Floors	_____	_____	_____
Steps	_____	_____	_____
Sidewalks and driveways	_____	_____	_____
Patios	_____	_____	_____
Septic tank	_____	_____	_____
Swimming pool	_____	_____	_____
Culverts and drains	_____	_____	_____
Bridges	_____	_____	_____
Parging**	_____	_____	_____
Emulsion	_____	_____	_____
Insulation board	_____	_____	_____
Foundation Subtotal			_____

*pier pads are concrete support pads whose size varies with the load
**parging is the plastering of concrete (or concrete block) walls before applying emulsion

Item	Estimate	Quote	Totals
FLOOR SYSTEMS			
Posts and columns	_____	_____	_____
Beams and girders	_____	_____	_____
Termite shield	_____	_____	_____
Sill plates	_____	_____	_____
Joists	_____	_____	_____
Joist hangers	_____	_____	_____
Headers	_____	_____	_____
Bridging	_____	_____	_____
Subfloor	_____	_____	_____
Floor Systems Subtotal			_____
EXTERIOR WALLS			
Pre-built shell	_____	_____	_____
Wall logs	_____	_____	_____
Porch and deck logs	_____	_____	_____
Exterior Walls Subtotal			_____
ROOF LOGS			
Gable-end-logs	_____	_____	_____
Trusses	_____	_____	_____
Purlins	_____	_____	_____
Rafters	_____	_____	_____
Bracing	_____	_____	_____
Roof sheathing	_____	_____	_____
Flashing	_____	_____	_____
Building paper	_____	_____	_____
Roofing felt	_____	_____	_____
Shingles	_____	_____	_____
Metal roofing	_____	_____	_____
Exterior finish and trim	_____	_____	_____
Fascia, soffit and molding	_____	_____	_____
Gutter and downspout	_____	_____	_____
Roof Logs Subtotal			_____

Item	Estimate	Quote	Totals
FIREPLACE AND CHIMNEY			
Footing	_____	_____	_____
Bricks	_____	_____	_____
Concrete block	_____	_____	_____
Mortar and fire-clay*	_____	_____	_____
Flue lining	_____	_____	_____
Damper	_____	_____	_____
Clean-out	_____	_____	_____
Fuel chute	_____	_____	_____
Ash dump	_____	_____	_____
Chimney cap	_____	_____	_____
Flashing	_____	_____	_____
Insulation	_____	_____	_____
Hearth	_____	_____	_____
Fireplace and Chimney Subtotal			_____
WINDOWS			
Cut to size and sanding	_____	_____	_____
Rough frame	_____	_____	_____
Flashing	_____	_____	_____
Window sash	_____	_____	_____
Windows Subtotal			_____
EXTERIOR DOORS			
Cut to size and sanding	_____	_____	_____
Frame	_____	_____	_____
Flashing	_____	_____	_____
Front door	_____	_____	_____
Back door	_____	_____	_____
Side or balcony doors	_____	_____	_____
Patio doors	_____	_____	_____
Garage doors	_____	_____	_____
Storm and screen doors	_____	_____	_____
Exterior Doors Subtotal			_____

*fire-proof mortar

Item	Estimate	Quote	Totals
INTERIOR DOORS			
Room doors	_____	_____	_____
Closets	_____	_____	_____
Linen closet	_____	_____	_____
Storage	_____	_____	_____
Attic	_____	_____	_____
Interior Doors Subtotal			_____
INTERIOR WALLS			
Log walls	_____	_____	_____
Stud walls	_____	_____	_____
Drywall	_____	_____	_____
Paneling	_____	_____	_____
Interior Walls Subtotal			_____
SECOND FLOOR			
Posts and columns	_____	_____	_____
Beams and girders	_____	_____	_____
Joists	_____	_____	_____
Joist hangers	_____	_____	_____
Headers and bridging	_____	_____	_____
Second Floor Subtotal			_____
STAIRS			
Interior			
Basement	_____	_____	_____
Second floor	_____	_____	_____
Attic	_____	_____	_____
Exterior			
Stairs	_____	_____	_____
Handrails and balustrades	_____	_____	_____
Stairs Subtotal			_____
HEATING AND AIR-CONDITIONING			
Heating equipment	_____	_____	_____
Cooling equipment	_____	_____	_____
Thermostat	_____	_____	_____
Heat exchanger	_____	_____	_____
Humidifier	_____	_____	_____
Dehumidifier	_____	_____	_____
Air filter	_____	_____	_____
Heating and Air-Conditioning Subtotal			_____

Item	Estimate	Quote	Totals
INTERIOR FINISHING			
Floor deadening underlay	_____	_____	_____
Flooring finish	_____	_____	_____
Hardwood	_____	_____	_____
Carpet	_____	_____	_____
Padding	_____	_____	_____
Tile, resilient	_____	_____	_____
Tile, ceramic	_____	_____	_____
Brick, stone, slate baseboard	_____	_____	_____
Wall molding and chair rail	_____	_____	_____
Window and door trim	_____	_____	_____
Closet shelves and hardware	_____	_____	_____
Door locks, handles and hinges	_____	_____	_____
Ceiling finish	_____	_____	_____
Painting	_____	_____	_____
Wallpapering	_____	_____	_____
Cabinets, fixtures and appliances	_____	_____	_____
Interior Finishing Subtotal			_____
KITCHEN			
Oven and range	_____	_____	_____
Refrigerator	_____	_____	_____
Icemaker	_____	_____	_____
Sink	_____	_____	_____
Dishwasher	_____	_____	_____
Garbage disposal	_____	_____	_____
Trash compactor	_____	_____	_____
Microwave	_____	_____	_____
Food processor	_____	_____	_____
Exhaust fan	_____	_____	_____
Cabinets	_____	_____	_____
Countertop	_____	_____	_____
Kitchen Subtotal			_____

Item	Estimate	Quote	Totals
BATHROOMS			
Toilets	_____	_____	_____
Bathtubs	_____	_____	_____
Showers	_____	_____	_____
Whirlpool	_____	_____	_____
Saunas	_____	_____	_____
Sinks	_____	_____	_____
Medicine cabinet	_____	_____	_____
Countertops	_____	_____	_____
Towel bars	_____	_____	_____
Soap holders	_____	_____	_____
Paper holders	_____	_____	_____
Bath and shower rails	_____	_____	_____
Tile floor and walls	_____	_____	_____
Mirrors	_____	_____	_____
Bathrooms Subtotal			_____
LAUNDRY			
Washer and dryer	_____	_____	_____
Sink	_____	_____	_____
Water softener	_____	_____	_____
Water heater	_____	_____	_____
Laundry Subtotal			_____
FINISH AND CLEANUP			
Fine grading	_____	_____	_____
Landscaping	_____	_____	_____
Seeding and planting	_____	_____	_____
Interior cleaning and polishing	_____	_____	_____
Trash removal	_____	_____	_____
Finish and Cleanup Subtotal			_____
MOVE-IN			
Occupancy permit	_____	_____	_____
Power, water, phone hook-up	_____	_____	_____
Moving expenses	_____	_____	_____
Move-in Subtotal			_____
TOTAL			_____

CHAPTER 6

STARTING A LOG HOUSE

Starting a log house is the easiest part of the whole undertaking. Getting ready to build and finishing the house after the roof is on is often harder, but starting is quite straightforward. In simpler days when it was not required to do all the planning and site preparation that I have been talking about, it was even easier to get started than it is now. The foundation would consist of several big rocks that were close to level and the first two stout logs would carry the floor. We have now become more urbane with our building foundations and would find it hard to manage without a basement. But there was a time when the most beautiful basements and foundations were built of rock. I would not totally abandon the idea.

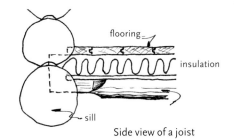

Side view of a joist

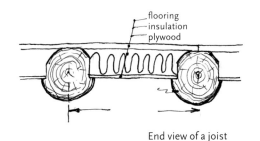

End view of a joist

Two views of an insulated floor.

A simple house start with a rock foundation and floor joists suspended in first round, an old and honorable way to start a log house. This is how I built Knotingham at Shanty Lake.

A full stonework foundation might be undertaken by an experienced stonemason.

Building the Foundation

You, however, will have a concrete foundation, and, in the case of the design that I have chosen, Plan 793 from *Log House Plans*, you will also have a concrete floor. To build this foundation, start with a site leveled for at least two meters beyond the building line. If fill is required, it must be compacted to avoid settling, and if the site is low, it can be raised with compacted fill. The pilings, treated wood or concrete posts, can be dug into the undisturbed site or, if fill is employed, they may be set on ground level and filled to grade. A reinforced concrete grade beam is poured on the top of the posts. Place J-bolts at two-meter intervals to anchor the first round of logs. This beam, as an alternative, may be notched and carry a regular wood floor, or you can pour an insulated concrete floor. If a concrete floor is chosen, water, sewer and electrical must be provided in an accessible manner before the floor is placed. For this reason, many prefer to build an insulated wood floor.

You may also choose to build a concrete basement. This would be formed in the same way any other building is done, then building a floor on top before constructing the house. However, another more satisfying foundation may be made with stone.

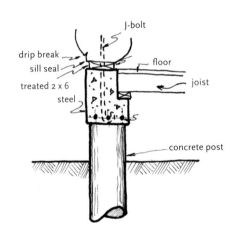

Grade beam notch to accept an insulated wood floor.

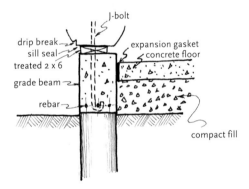

Grade beam with concrete floor.

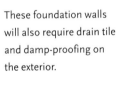

These foundation walls will also require drain tile and damp-proofing on the exterior.

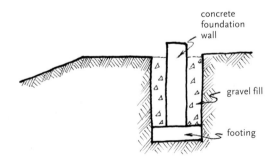

Concrete posts may be dug down below the frost line to a footing.

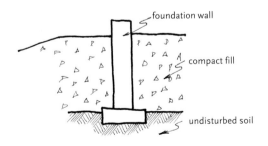

The footing can be placed higher and the required depth obtained with fill.

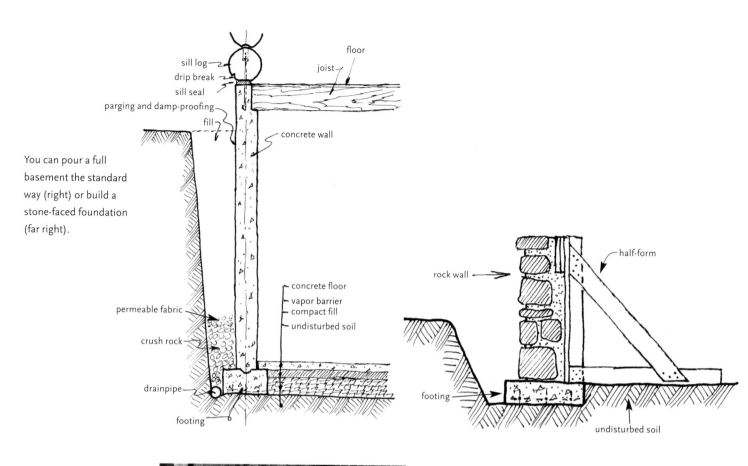

sill log

drip break

sill seal

parging and damp-proofing

fill

floor

joist

concrete wall

You can pour a full
basement the standard
way (right) or build a
stone-faced foundation
(far right).

permeable fabric

crush rock

drainpipe

footing

concrete floor

vapor barrier

compact fill

undisturbed soil

rock wall

half-form

footing

undisturbed soil

Rock facing on the
foundation wall
improves the
appearance.

A good method for beginners is to use a partial form and build the rockwork against this background. Use a footing specified for the ground conditions on the site, then build a one-sided foundation form on the inside of the wall. Once you have obtained a suitable supply of rock, there are two important rules for doing rockwork. Rocks must be laid on a level bed across the wall and the join between any two rocks should be broken, or bridged, with the next course. Do not build too high in one place and keep the mortar line plumb. Wood wedges can be employed to secure difficult stones, and a movable grid, about 60 cm high and 240 cm long, made of 6-8 mm rod, can make the job easier.

Mix mortar in a "boat" made of sheet metal. The mix should be about one to three parts masonry cement and sand. You will soon learn what is a good mix and just how rigid it should be. The mortar can be improved by adding a portion of Portland cement to the mix. The mortar will be stronger and more waterproof but it will be more difficult to handle and will set up much faster. Use this only after you have become skilful. Practise on a different wall or at least some place out of sight. Your skill will improve rapidly to a level you will be proud of.

Your site is now ready and the first day of real building is about to start. I have not yet talked about the tools you will need throughout the project and I will not do so here. Nor, in my enthusiasm to get started, have I talked about peeling the logs. See Chapter 7.

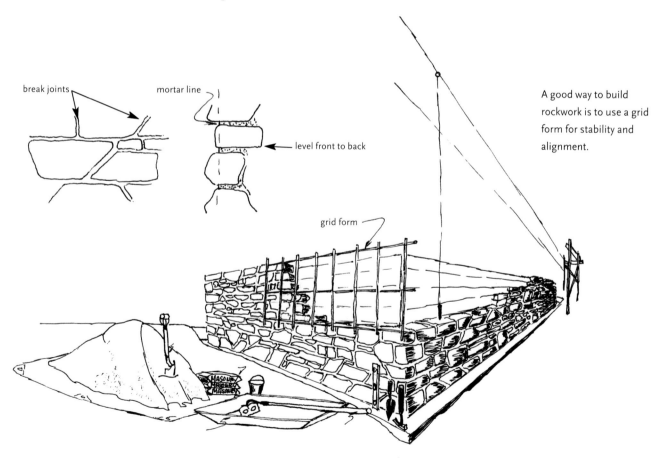

break joints

mortar line

level front to back

grid form

A good way to build rockwork is to use a grid form for stability and alignment.

The First Logs

I am going to assume that you will be building on your foundation rather than on another location. This is because you are using hand methods as much as is possible, and while it is in many ways desirable to build on an off-site location, you do not wish to move logs twice by hand.

The first log or logs are chosen with form and size in mind. Because this building is square, it matters little which walls are to receive the first logs. Let's say it's the two sides of the building, the sides parallel to the fireplace. Choose a log that is near straight and slightly larger than the average. Most likely you will split this log in two with a chainsaw and use a blind notch at the ends. This is the most usual way because one log will do the work of two.

There is another way to do this if you would rather work only with hand tools. Choose two logs that are less than the average size and hew them flat on the bottom where they will be in contact with the foundation. The logs can be hewn with only an axe if it has a good pattern, such as a swamping axe pattern. The axe "pattern" describes the size and shape of the tool. For example, a swamping axe is intended for general use and has a wider face than a felling axe, but is narrower than a hewing axe. The sides of the face are symmetrical, while a hewing axe is flat on one side. Each of these axes is further differentiated by the range of sizes it is available in. Possibly a better job might be done with a crosscut saw and a hewing axe. Whichever method you decide on, flatten the log to a thickness that will leave material to about half the diameter of the log that will be placed on it. If the next log is slightly larger than the average, this should be easy.

Which way around the first logs are placed does not matter as far as the logistics of log placement are concerned. They may be placed with the large ends in one direction or in opposite directions. By the time you have reached the top of the windows or the roof overhang, it may be advantageous to have both large ends pointing the same direction. It is therefore often decided to place the first two logs with the butts the same way.

In order to hew the first logs flat on the underside, place them first on two cross-

The professional way to rip the first log in two.

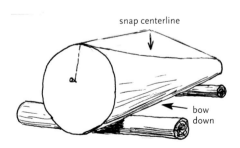

snap centerline

bow down

Two plumb lines 20 mm apart centered on ink line (centerline) each end.

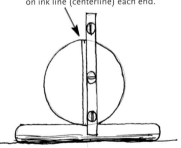

Cut lines originating with plumb lines. Keep the saw between the lines.

10 mm

sleepers so that any bend of bow in the log is downward in the center. This will place the straightest aspect to either side, one of which may be selected for the cut. Fix the log firmly in place and snap a chalkline straight down onto the top of the log at a location that will give you the dimension that you have chosen. Draw plumb lines from the ends of this chalkline onto the ends of the log and join these lines with another chalkline after your log has been rolled 180 degrees (Fig. 1). Again roll the log 90 degrees until the side to be hewn is upward. Locate the center of the log length and measure back half the length of the wall plus about 12 mm and make a saw cut to the chalklines. Do the same at each end. This will leave a round portion at the ends (Fig. 2). Now make saw cuts down to the lines each 150 to 200 mm apart along the length to be flattened. This is called "scoring" the log (Fig. 3). These segments can be split off and the surface cut straight and true to the line.

Most of the work should be done with an ordinary axe. Cut downward and across the grain to avoid splitting the wood and take care to hit neither the ground or your feet, for the axe must be very sharp. Hold the axe handle close to the head for this work, about 300 mm. And keep both hands close together as you would if you were playing golf and for the same reason: you can not be accurate if your hands are apart (Fig. 4). The final product may be brought into better alignment with a slick or finished still further with a hand plane, if such a degree of refinement is required (Fig 5).

Steps for hewing the first log flat.

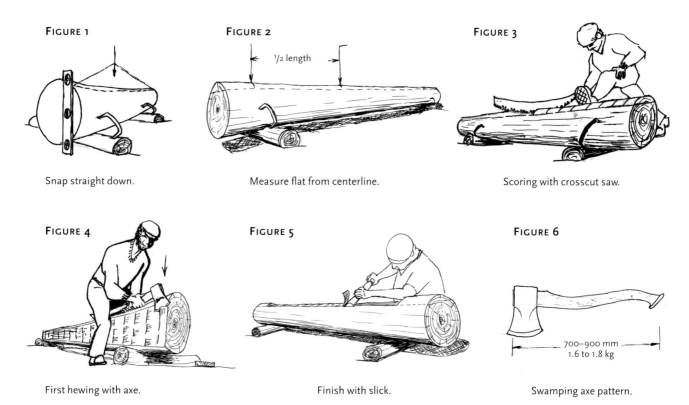

FIGURE 1

Snap straight down.

FIGURE 2

½ length

Measure flat from centerline.

FIGURE 3

Scoring with crosscut saw.

FIGURE 4

First hewing with axe.

FIGURE 5

Finish with slick.

FIGURE 6

700–900 mm
1.6 to 1.8 kg

Swamping axe pattern.

Two ways to cut a drip break:

A chainsaw groove on the underside of the log.

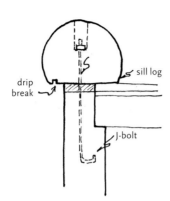

A lip cut where the flat is too narrow.

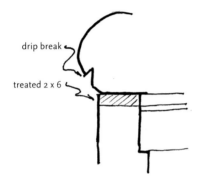

Use a strip of flashing in the sill log for the drip break.

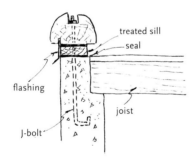

A through-bolt anchor that can be adjusted. A metal box in the foundation allows access to adjust bolt.

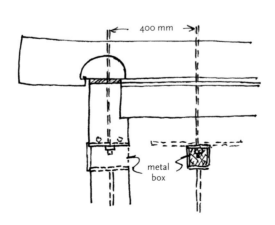

At this point the flat portion of the log is up and you can place a centerline on it. This line, which will become the center of the wall, should be equal distant from the edge of the flat and generally near the center of the log. Sometimes this may not be possible and you will have to make the best compromise you can. Place a second line parallel to this centerline for the drip break. The drip break will be a shallow groove just outside the foundation line, so that any driven water that runs down the wall will not work its way under the wall. The best way to install a drip break is to make a shallow (20 mm) cut along the foundation line with an electric saw. When the log is in its final position on the building, a flashing can be inserted into this cut that will extend over the sill pad and onto the concrete.

The only work now needed on these two logs, before they are placed in their final position, is to drill them for anchor bolts and through-bolts. Most building authorities require that the first log be bolted to the foundation.

I have not been convinced of the necessity for these bolts in all instances. Perhaps their purpose is to provide a start for your replacement house if this one is washed away with high water. The bolting is accomplished by carefully placing J-bolts along the centerline and drilling the first log accordingly. These holes can be laid out along the centerline and drilled oversize to ensure an easy fit. The through-bolts at the end should be set up to allow retensioning from the bottom.

Placing the Logs

This first round of logwork can often be put into position by hand. If the location allows, it may be possible to place several rounds of logs before you have to call for power to move the logs up. By the use of skids, peavey (a lever for moving and rolling logs) and rope line, you can roll the first two logs onto the building. Naturally it would help if the log supply was uphill from the building, but that is not really necessary.

Place the skids firmly against the wall and even fasten them in place. Position the first log at the bottom of these poles and rig the ropes with the bitter end (the end that is secured) inside the building and lead the working end around the log from underneath as shown in the sketch. Two men can roll a large log up a considerable grade onto a building by this means. Just remember that the butt end will move further than the top end with each revolution and must therefore start further down the skid. Because this log is flat on one side, it

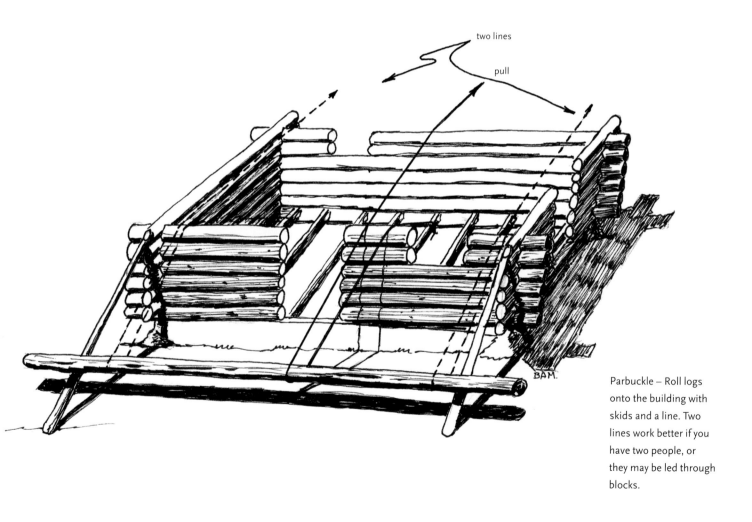

two lines

pull

Parbuckle – Roll logs onto the building with skids and a line. Two lines work better if you have two people, or they may be led through blocks.

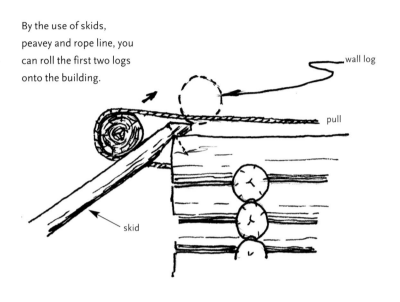

By the use of skids, peavey and rope line, you can roll the first two logs onto the building.

wall log

pull

skid

Block the logs up into position for the first round.

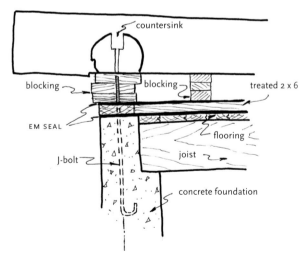

countersink

blocking

blocking

treated 2 x 6

EM SEAL

flooring

J-bolt

joist

concrete foundation

will not roll easily. For this reason you may wish to place it up onto the floor before it is flattened. If it has been flattened first, one man with a peavey will have to ease it over the turn each time.

Go slowly to avoid accidents and remember that you want the bow of the log to the outside. At this time, you will have placed a plank of treated wood (40 x 150 mm) around the perimeter of the floor on top of the foundation (see illustration). Now staple a gasket seal on top of this plank and put the first log in place. A good way to position this log over the sill bolts is to ramp it up onto a stack of short blocks until it is as high as the bolt tops, slide it into the right spot, then remove the blocking one end at a time. The first log should slide obediently into place and your log house is off to a first-class start.

Place the other logs the same way, each with the bow out. Replace the skids at the end of these logs and roll the next two logs up onto the top. These will also have to be flattened in much the same manner as the first, then positioned directly over the final location they are to occupy. By this time all the bolt holes are drilled and you are ready to scribe and fit the first notches.

*The backhoe (left) was an
important part of the work crew,
which helped the walls fly up.*

*Cutting the fine finishing curve on
a saddle notch (below).*

I used the backhoe to clear the snow off Paul's site, put down two old logs
for skids and decked the twenty-eight building logs. I put the temporary
building foundation posts on pads because the ground was frozen. These
pads were moved into a very accurate location but the posts were left long,
to be cut to the right size later. I poured water around them and left them
to freeze overnight.

   The next morning I used a water level (filled with windshield-washer
fluid) to strike a level line around the four squared posts. I checked these
carefully with the carpenter level after they had been sawn off. They should
be level from any direction. That the posts be level is a little more important than that they be perfect to height, although there is no reason that
they can't be both. I snapped the centerline on one side with an ink line
because this prints a thinner line than a chalkline does, but you have to
keep it warm in cold weather. If you know the diagonal measurement of
the building, it is easy to pick out the third and fourth corners by using two
tapes. If you don't know the length of the diagonal, just check that they are
equal. I did that anyway, just to be sure. I snapped on the four centerlines

Brushing the first half-logs flat (below).
Fraser scribing for the notch (bottom).

across the posts and cut these into the posts with a handsaw so that they could not be lost and so they could be seen from the side.

I would like to have done this house completely with an axe but a chainsaw is a tremendous temptation when the logs are hard and dry and you have to maximize the material. I chose my first log and split it in two. These first half-logs were brushed flat with the chainsaw, marked with a centerline, a line for the drip break, a length line and a reference line at right angles to the centerline, placed 500 mm back from the length line. I picked these logs up with a pair of tongs attached to the hoe and set them down as near the proper position as I could judge. Now they had to be pushed and pried into the accurate location. That is why the pads were frozen in solidly – so that all my accurate work would stay in place.

These first half-logs were across the short ends of the building. I picked out the two longer sill logs to make the three-quarter sill, flattened these with the chainsaw and lifted them into position. I used blind dovetail notches for the four corners. I always do this because I think it is the best notch for this location. It takes a little practice to do it right but not any longer than any other notch so, why not?

The rest was comparatively easy. It was now the middle of April and the days were warmer as well as longer. I was working alone but not in

isolation. Paul was also working on the site or he was not too far away. We had a work bee one weekend where I was helped by Paul and my son-in-law, Fraser Jackson. That weekend the house shot on up and the walls were finished by the first week in May.

It is a temptation to bypass a lot of the preparatory work when your house is a long way from the final site and a long way from completion. By preparatory work I mean the cutting of window and door headers and making the cutouts for upper floor or loft flooring. It is also especially important to make the plate cuts on the outriggers and the slope cuts for the roof structure. These must be done when the plates and other members are being put in place. To bypass this work seems to save time and effort, but it will cost more time and work later and the quality of the work will be compromised. Why not do this work while the building is being disassembled or reassembled? Yes, it can be done at those times but most likely you will have hired a crew and equipment for these jobs and time will be even more pressing to get the job done to schedule.

Finished walls, ready to move to the final site.

CHAPTER 7

GOOD SITE, GOOD TOOLS, GOOD WORK

By now you will feel that your building has truly been started. It's a good feeling and it is easy to count the few days that it will take to finish the walls and put on the roof. From this time on, I expect that progress on the building will be steady and orderly, and in line with the work schedule. There are two topics that I have not yet discussed that should be fully considered before we go any further. One is the work site you will use and the other is the collection of tools and equipment you will need.

THE WORK SITE

Most buildings are built off of the foundation and this is generally a good practice. Because you are building by hand, however, you may choose to work right on the permanent location, providing the foundation is not too high and the site is clear and level.

On the other hand, there are also good reasons to work off the foundation even if you are building without power equipment. Your per-manent site may not be ready, or it may be too steep or too far away, or it may have some other drawback that makes it awkward to work on. After all, your permanent location was chosen as a place to live and may not necessarily be a desirable place to work.

A good work site will overcome many of the disadvantages of a difficult house location and can be rented or leased for the building process. Such a building site should be level, clear and large enough to accommodate the building, log supply, tools and equipment as well as the bark, sawdust and other debris occasioned by the work on the building. Building off of the foundation is a well-established practise and many builders would not think of working any other way. Disassembling the building and rebuilding it on the foundation requires renting a crane for only a short period. This can pay off in time saved and ease of construction. In this case, however, you will be doing your building right on the foundation and each log will be finished and in its final position when you are through with it.

Even though you are building on the foundation, good site planning will make the job go much better. The logs will be piled to one end of the lot and on the high side if possible. The logs will be raised above the ground on sleepers (skid logs) so that they are off the ground and more easily rolled. Build, or move in, a small tool shed and place it out of the way. On some sites this may simply be a strong table with a roof over it. If you are using a truck crane, it can be placed in the middle of the floor. Because you will be rolling logs, putting it in the center would not be practical, so it will have to be placed to the side.

Even if you have a shed for security, the work table can be very handy for the day's activity. If electricity is available, put up a temporary power pole as close to the building as is practical. Although you are mostly working by hand, some electrical tools do provide a welcome advantage.

Work site layout
1) Access
2) Project
3) Lift truck
4) Log selection
5) Peeling rack
6) Delivery
7) Log pile
8) Bark
9) Toilet
10) Tool security
11) Lunch shelter
12) Tool shelter
13) Sawdust pile
14) Waste bin

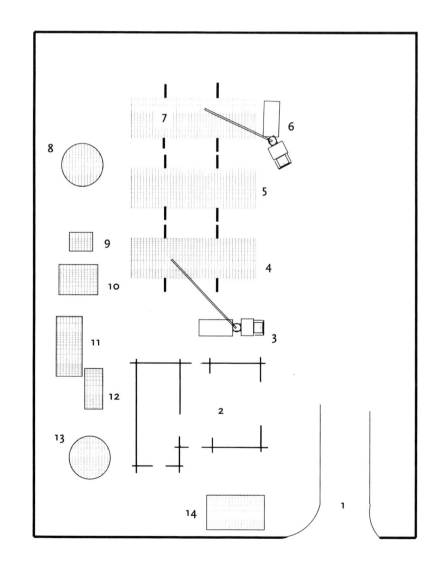

PEELING THE LOGS

Peel all the logs. It is a lot of work: as much work, perhaps, as building the walls. But it is a good idea to have all the logs peeled up before you start so that they are less liable to insect attack and the choice of the next log does not depend on which logs are peeled. This work can be delegated to someone else. For instance, students are well suited to this as a piecework undertaking. But do a good part of it yourself; there is satisfaction to be gained by doing this work. There is no easy way for the individual to peel logs by hand but it is a great way to get into shape!

Roll the log out onto the skids at a comfortable height and use the drawknife or peeling spud. I prefer the drawknife. If the logs are cut, as they should be, in the winter or late summer, the bark will be firmly fixed to the wood. If the logs are cut and peeled in the spring or early summer, the bark will come off easily but the quality of the wood will be greatly diminished.

Logs that are cut in the winter will still peel easily for a few days at some point in the spring. If you are able to monitor the material and fit your schedule into that time frame, the work will be easier.

If the logs have been cut for some time and the bark is dried on, it sometimes helps to wet them down with a sprinkler for a few hours in order to soften the bark. You will end up with a lot of bark. If the logs are to be stored on the skids, this material should be removed for sanitation reasons, because it is in a condition that will encourage insect populations.

As previously stated, there is no magic formula that will remove bark from a log. True, there are power-driven mechanical debarkers,

Peeling white pine logs on the skids.

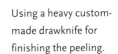

Using a heavy custom-made drawknife for finishing the peeling.

Cotton from nearby cottonwood trees looks like snow on peeled logs.

but I have always placed these things high on the list of obscenities that we are forever inflicting on the trees. High pressure water is an alternative, but again, you have decided to work by hand.

I am often asked the question, "How difficult is it?" One of the great joys in undertaking a log building, especially if the work is done by hand, is that of placing yourself in direct association with the environment. To avoid any part of the process is therefore to deprive yourself of the satisfaction you are seeking. This does not mean that you must make everything as difficult as possible, but rather that you discover the truth of each undertaking and learn to work with that. This way, that which was difficult becomes just another challenge to be welcomed.

When peeling either with a peeling spud or a heavy drawknife, it is a good idea to first remove all the knots as close to the line of the tree trunk as is possible. This is best done with a heavier axe because sometimes a large knot is quite tough and requires a hard blow. As is always the case, the tools must be kept very sharp, because if they are not sharp, the work will be difficult, poorly done and dangerous.

If the logs are to be peeled any length of time before the building is undertaken, they should be sheltered and treated with a mild preservative (Fig. 1). The log may be rolled on down the skid until it is well off the ground and several tiers built up so that a temporary roof can be placed over them. The logs should not touch and they should be coated with a mild fungicide, such as borax or oxalic acid. The use of strong chemicals could be very dangerous to the builder later on. The spacers used between the tiers should be kept directly on top of the sleepers and the logs should be rotated until the bow is up. When the time to start building comes, it may be necessary to again spread the logs out onto the skids because the best log for immediate use will often be right on the bottom of the pile.

FIGURE 1

MOVING THE LOGS

Moving logs by hand will require care and planning. Most of us think in terms of using power of some kind and I think that this is not unreasonable. Even buying a hydraulic crane truck with the intention of reselling it after the job is completed is not unreasonable. The first log house I built for my family on the shore of François Lake in northern British Columbia was built entirely by hand. The site was too wet and soft to be able to use machinery, but more to the point, I could not in any way afford to buy or hire any such assistance. I moved the logs and put them up on the walls by hand. The logs were moved with wood rollers on planks and parbuckled onto the wall with a block and tackle (Fig. 2). This is hard work to the point where it might be called punishment, but the only cost was time and energy, each of which I had in abundance.

A two-wheeled pole mover is also an option if the ground is hard and level (Fig. 3). This is a two-wheeled cart with an arched axle. It has a reach fastened to the top of this axle. The reach has a short end and a long end. In operation, the long end is lifted and the short end chained to near the balance point of the log. The long end is then pulled down and secured. The log is thereby lifted off the ground.

A better system is a skyline. This is an overhead cable system which may span both the

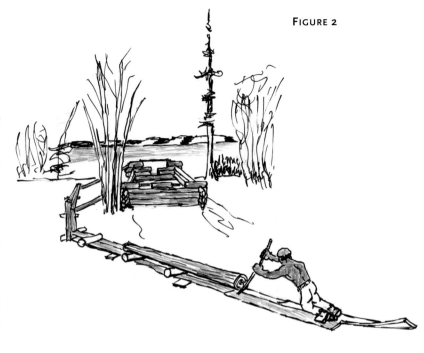

FIGURE 2

FIGURE 3

Students putting a building up by hand with the help of a skyline.

log deck and the building. A skyline setup can be operated with a chain hoist, a come-along, a vehicle or a winch. Here, unless one is a purist bordering on fanaticism, the use of an electric- or gasoline-powered winch could be still considered hand operation. The trees or upright logs used for each end of the skyline should be at least 10 m above the ground and large enough to be totally safe. Use a sound log at least 12 m long with a 250 mm top, the butt end of which has been set 2 m into the ground. These poles should be guyed with at least three 12-mm cables that are securely fastened to stumps or anchor logs and the skyline itself should be 16 mm to 19 mm steel cable, properly installed with tree irons. I must insist that an experienced rigger should be employed, or at least consulted, for this setup because the proper splices and fastenings are most important. Ask around for a good rigger or look one up in the phone book.

If the logs can be rolled out of the pile and then up to the wall, a floor hoist is a very practical device. This is a wheeled dolly on the floor

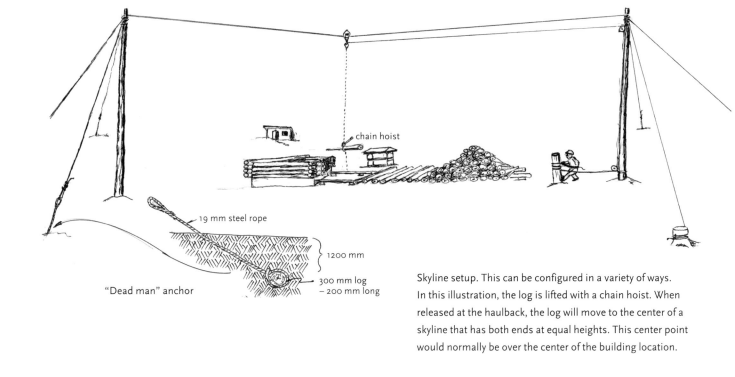

chain hoist

19 mm steel rope

1200 mm

"Dead man" anchor

300 mm log – 200 mm long

Skyline setup. This can be configured in a variety of ways. In this illustration, the log is lifted with a chain hoist. When released at the haulback, the log will move to the center of a skyline that has both ends at equal heights. This center point would normally be over the center of the building location.

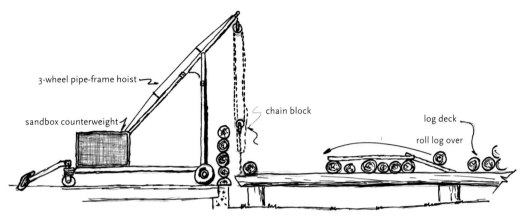

3-wheel pipe-frame hoist

sandbox counterweight

chain block

log deck

roll log over

A well-made floor hoist can be a safe and handy way to move logs. In order that this setup be safe, equipment, connections and operation should be inspected by an experienced rigger.

that can reach over the wall and hoist a log. Then both log and hoist can be pushed to the desired location. If it is made in such a manner that it may be taken apart and reassembled on an upper floor, it will also serve to build the roof structure. Even if the logs are moved to the building with a skyline, the floor hoist is still a practical consideration for placing the logs on the wall, because the skyline will not reach all the walls.

Another method of placing logs is what is called a "gin pole." This is a guyed derrick that may be placed inside the house or near the wall. Using a hand or electric winch, it raises logs and swings them into the wall. Before you build this, you must employ or consult a rigger or engineer.

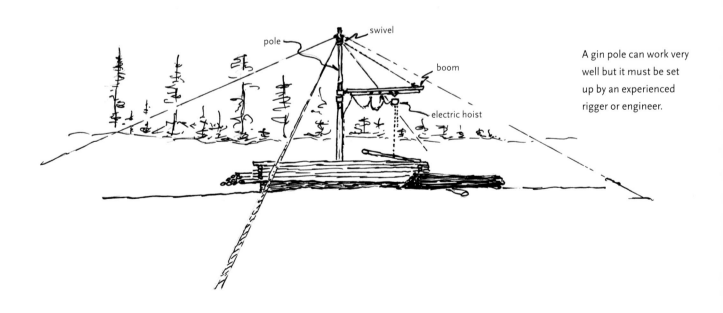

pole

swivel

boom

electric hoist

A gin pole can work very well but it must be set up by an experienced rigger or engineer.

SAFETY

Now that you are dealing with heavy logs, machines, cable systems and lifting devices, some thought should be given to safety.

Logs

These are heavy things and even a medium-sized log may weigh as much as a ton. Never be downgrade from an unsecured log and never stand or even pass under a suspended log: go around. Roll logs inward on the wall and always be aware of your perimeter while you work. Make sure that the log is always under control and secured with log dogs.

Tools and Equipment

It goes without saying that hand tools should be sharp and in good order and that equipment must be in good repair. In particular, this applies to axes and peaveys. If they are dull, or if the handles are incorrect, they can be dangerous. Cables, hoists, blocks and lines on hoisting equipment should be inspected periodically by an experienced rigger.

Chainsaws

Chainsaw use will be restricted to cutting off the end of logs but they are a hand-held tool and safe use is imperative. Maintain the saw and chain according to the manufacturer's instructions. Start the saw by placing it on the ground with your foot on the pad or else by securing the handle at the throttle end, between your legs. Never drop start a chainsaw. Make sure that there is no one close to you. Find out what causes "kickback" and keep your left thumb around the handle bar. These are a few of the considerations, but a chainsaw is as dangerous as a shotgun, and for the new or inexperienced operator, I must recommend at least basic coaching or instruction before this machine is used. Safety clothing should also be part of the required equipment. This will consist of hard hat and gloves and, with a chainsaw, include chainsaw pants or chaps and ear and eye protection.

First Aid

First-aid materials should also be at hand. The most common need will be for small cuts and a supply of Band-Aids will do the job. Larger cuts and fractures will, I hope, not happen, but just in case, the first-aid kit should include field dressings, splints and bandages and the builder should know how to use them. Avoid working alone or in isolation and have a plan of action in case of emergency.

THE ESSENTIAL TOOLS ARE:

- axe: swamping pattern, 1.6 to 1.8 kg (3.5 to 4 lbs)
- peavey
- chainsaw or crosscut saw
- scribers
- carpenter's level: 60 cm (2 ft)
- flexible square
- chalkline

- chisels: heavy, 35 mm wide (1 1/2 in); curved, 25 mm (1 in) #1 curve
- tape measure: 10 m (33 ft)
- drawknife: heavy
- slick
- pencil, lumber crayon
- log dogs

TOOLS

The tools required to build a log house by hand are not extensive, nor are they expensive. Indeed one can carry all the most necessary tools in one trip from the tool shed to the job site. Beyond this basic set, you can become as elaborate and get as expensive as you wish.

Of these tools, the axes will require the most attention to bring to a good edge. This is accomplished by first grinding the axe head to the right shape, then honing the edge until it is both sharp and tough. For logwork, the shape shown in the illustration is the most satisfactory. If the edge is too thin, it can be damaged by hard knots. If the axe were to be used as a racing axe, the edge could be straighter and thinner because the wood used for this sport is selected to be free of knots.

Grinding and honing an axe can be done with an angle grinder equipped first with a grinding disk and then with a sanding disk. Some axes are too hard to use a file on but others can be brought to a final shape by the use of a 250 mm flat file. Next use a water stone of 800 grit, then bring the axe to a high polish with increasingly finer stones. The final edge can be honed with a 2000-grit stone.

The edges of the drawknife and the chisels are fashioned in about the same way. A little practice will soon provide you with a tool that cuts clean and easily and time spent learning this skill is time well spent. I am reluctant to describe here the techniques of sharpening a crosscut or snab saw. This requires special tools and skill that is best taught by demonstration. If you are fortunate enough to own such a saw, I would suggest that you take it to the nearest saw filer and ask to be shown this skill.

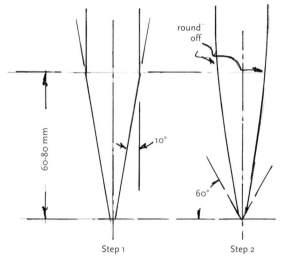

An axe must be properly sharpened for use on a building. Use an angle grinder to obtain the best shape, then finish with hand stones. Take care not to burn the edge.

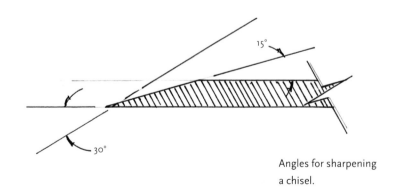

Angles for sharpening a chisel.

A useful set of axes. Left to right: Oxhead, Arvika and broadaxe.

TOOLS FOR MARKING, MOVING, CUTTING

- Mackie scriber
- log dog
- broadaxe
- Starret scriber
- Arvika axe
- chalkline
- peavey
- Oxhead axe
- felt marker
- crosscut saw
- pencil
- chisel – 35 mm (1 1/2 in)
- tape measure – 10 m (33 ft)
- curve chisel
- slick
- scarf board
- drawknife
- flexible square
- gouge knife
- level
- chainsaw

A peavey is indispensable: you will use it as much as your tape measure.

Rolling log dogs can either hold the log steady or allow it to roll.

Cutting logs to clear the right-of-way into Shanty Lake.

SHANTY LAKE

THE ROAD

Knotingham, or at least the walls, was finished. The next job would be to move it to the site. This would require the building of two miles of road. I thought I knew quite a bit about building roads, but like logs, different locations can present different characteristics. I remembered some comments made by the British and American military during the Second World War concerning the construction of the Burma road, and I thought of them often in the days to come.

I started by building a tote road – a rough pathway just wide enough to get the backhoe through. As I got further and further into the bush and swamps, I began to dread any kind of breakdown and the possible need to get heavy parts out for repair then back in again. I went back out and rebuilt the road to a better standard.

The spring was dry. According to people I met, it was maybe the driest on record. That was a bonus and I was able to put the trail right into the building site. I cleared a small area and decked the large white pine logs that had been skidded in during the winter for the construction of the

Land cruiser delivers fuel to the backhoe on the newly built tote road.

main house. It was still not possible to drive on the road. There were major wet spots. I did find a small amount of sand and carried this to some of the worst spots with the bucket on the front of the hoe. In the meantime we peeled the pine logs for the big house. I say "we" because the first weekend of peeling was a group project with friends and relatives joining in. Two four-wheel-drive vehicles made it as near as was possible, perhaps a little nearer than was wise. And we packed in the supplies of food, tents, sleeping bags, tools, tarps and fuel. We looked like one of those lines of European refugees struggling across some mountain range. It started to rain before we got the fire going.

The rain was a good thing because it wetted the logs that were beginning to dry and the next day Tony (a musician and family friend) and Fraser started peeling. The bark practically fell off and in the next two days we peeled sixty of the one hundred big pine logs. I used an old car spring cut in half for peeling spuds. A 150-mm piece of pipe welded at right angles on the inside of the curve provided a good purchase. The spring was ground thin at the cutting edge but not too sharp.

It rained, a lot, but one day the road dried enough so that I was able to drive in. For anyone that takes ready access to his house and out again to the grocery store for granted, this would be a revelation. This problem would not have been of any note to the early settler. A horse and wagon would not get stuck as easily as an old four-wheel drive and if it did get stuck, it could reasonably be taken apart and moved to solid ground. Now the time that had been devoted to packing everything across the mud holes was available for building. The days were long and sometimes it didn't even rain. Things moved right along. I decided that it was time to move Knotingham onto the site.

The road was still not passable for a large truck, but a single-axle boom truck could get within a mile. We chose a Saturday and loaded the top half of the building on the first load. This was brought to a wide spot along the road and off-loaded onto skids. A heavy downpour delayed the second load until the next morning, when the bottom half of the building was also put on the skids.

To move the building the rest of the way to the site required us to build a large two-wheeled trailer, which would be pulled by a rented skidder. A local welder made up the trailer from a large axle that I was able to supply. My neighbor across the lake owns an older skidder and one nice sunny weekend he drove it over. I thought I had just rented a skidder but along came the driver, two brothers and two friends, along with an extra tractor to load the logs. The day went exceptionally well and all the logs were on skids on my site by 4:00 p.m.

Skidder pulls precut Knotingham logs over the tote road.

CHAPTER 8

THE FIRST NOTCHES

With a safe and efficient work site organized and good tools in place, you can start fitting the first notches on the building. These first blind dovetail notches, done with hand tools, will be the most difficult. For this reason it would be a good idea to set up a practice situation for the first try.

BLIND DOVETAIL NOTCH

The log on the bottom (B) represents the smaller log that you have flattened and will have the dovetail tenon (Fig. 1). The upper log (A) will be the receiver and have the mortise cut. With the centerlines placed at 90 degrees (Fig. 2) (and over the center of the foundation when you come to work on the real thing), scribe the inside portion of the notch on the upper log (Fig. 2). The scriber setting will be the distance the flat on the upper log is above the flat on the lower log (Fig. 3), and the points and bubbles will have been carefully checked at the level board. Transfer the location of the

FIGURE 1

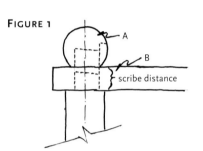

Set half-sill log (B) and three-quarter-sill log (A) on the foundation level, and plumb with center-lines intersecting at the center of the foundation.

FIGURE 2

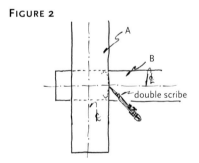

Scribe only the inside of the three-quarter log.

FIGURE 3

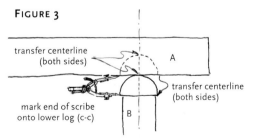

Transfer centerlines vertically from A to B and from B to A.

FIGURE 4

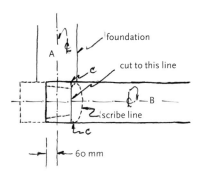

Roll the three-quarter log (A) in on the building, cut the half-sill log (B) 50-60 mm longer than the centerline on the foundation. Lay out and cut the dovetail.

FIGURE 5

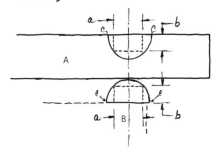

Cut the receiver to the scribe line on the three-quarter log (A), then lay out and cut the mortise.

FIGURE 6

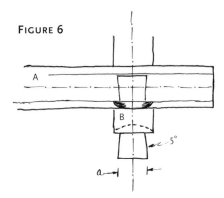

Check all the dimensions against its mate and then the blind dovetail is complete and ready to roll down.

centerlines from one log to the other (Fig. 3) and mark the location of the ends and center of the scribe on the lower log.

You are now ready to lay out and execute the cuts. Roll log A to the inside of the building and cut the end of the lower log 60 mm past the centerline (Fig. 4). Mark and place a centerline on this cut end that will join the top and bottom lengthwise lines (Fig. 5). Join the marks "c-c" across the top and you can lay out the dovetail measuring from the centerline "a" and terminating at the line "c-c." The sides and top of this tenon can be cut with a handsaw and the axe.

On the receiver, cut the round part of the notch to the scribe as deeply as to the bottom flat on the log (c-c) and at 90 degrees to the bottom, use your chisels. Again lay out the mortise from the centerlines to duplicate the tenon (Fig. 6). Part of the side cuts can be done with a handsaw and the cut finished with the flat chisel and the slick. Your notch should fit and you are ready to repeat the work on the building, and then your first round of logs will be in place.

After you have bolted this first round to the foundation, complete with drip breaks, sill seal, preservative treatment and pressure-treated spacer, you can move right into the long-awaited job of building the walls. By the time you are finished, this will seem like a simple and routine operation.

But until that time comes, be especially careful with the first logs, because if your work here is in any way below standard, later, when you have become more skilful, you may wish that you could do it over again.

SCARFS

Before you select and place the next logs onto the building, you will want to cut scarfs on the existing round of logs.

A scarf is a long, narrow wedge-shaped cut. The term is used to define the shallow cut on the top tangent of a log over which the next log will be fitted. The scarf, or flattened portion, is at an approximate 45-degree angle to the horizontal. The two flats will not meet at the top, rather, they will be separated by about 76 mm.

This is a little wider than the expected groove on the next log. They should extend a little below the top of the log underneath, about 18 mm, ideally, to the origin of the notch relief.

These cuts can be made with the axe and finished with a slick or a custom-made slick. The scarf can be one of several styles – use a template to do the layout so that they are all as uniform as possible. Be careful that you do not cut too deeply, for that is the most common mistake. The scarf is intended to help keep the notch fitting tightly as the log dries out (see illustration).

The notch you will be using is called a saddle notch, because of its shape. The scarf should reach only slightly below the anticipated location of the notch in the next log. If, because the next log is excessively crooked, it has to be cut deeper, then the scarf will have to be adjusted during the scribing process, but more on that later.

The style of scarf that is most often used is a slow sweep because it has the most natural look. Cut a shallow notch in the center and then slope in each side. If the axe is very sharp, the cut surface can be planed off smooth with the axe.

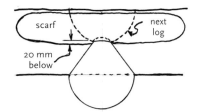

Scarf location.

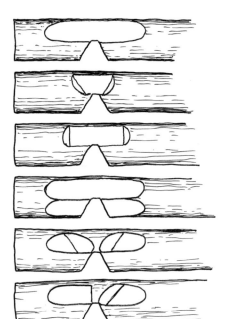

A wall log may be scarfed in one of several styles:

Long scarf

Scribed scarf

Square-cut scarf

Double-long scarf

Shrink-fitted scarf

Scarf with weather block in the center

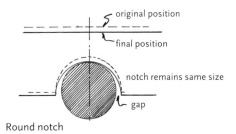

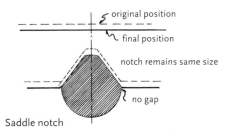

The scarfed notch will help reduce separation of the notch when the wood shrinks. The round notch may open up at the bottom.

Otherwise use a slick or a curved hand plane. The choice of tools will depend on the kind of wood that is being used. Cedar can be planed easily by hand, but Douglas fir is harder and most of the work would be done with an axe.

Log Selection

Log selection is the most demanding job on the building. If the logs are chosen correctly, the work will be easier and the building will look better. To do this well you must be familiar with your log supply and, of course, understand what you are trying to accomplish. Even-numbered rounds of logs (round two, four, six and so on) should end up near level on top and near the same height above the foundation.

Because logs are not perfectly straight, you will have to check the level by standing back a distance and sighting across your carpenter's level. Measure the height from the foundation at the center of the notch and note this figure on the log-end. It is generally better to use the larger logs near the bottom of the building and work into smaller logs as the structure goes up, but like all rules in log building, you will often make exceptions.

Place the chosen log on the building so that the large end is at the opposite end to that of the log below. This rule is also one that, on rare occasions, is broken. Because you have a strong concrete floor, use a floor hoist to move the log into position. When the log is in the approximate location, place log dogs in the rolling position and roll the log until the bow is outward and the top and bottom are as near straight as possible. If the log needs to be moved endways, reposition the hoist and lift again. Take care to place the material in the best possible position. Time spent to do this is not wasted and, indeed, may save a great deal of time later on.

Stand back and look at the log. Look from each end and look from the side. Are you pleased with it and do you feel satisfied that it is in the best position? If you are not, then change it until you are satisfied. If the log bows down in the center, it will require a deeper groove scribed into the center portion to obtain a fit. This will require a great deal of extra time and work to accomplish, but worse yet, the next log on top will have to be cut deeply at the ends. The result will then be a badly overcut notch and a possible loss of height. You will have done a lot of extra work to destroy expensive wood and to make the building less satisfactory. This is why it is necessary to take care in positioning each log.

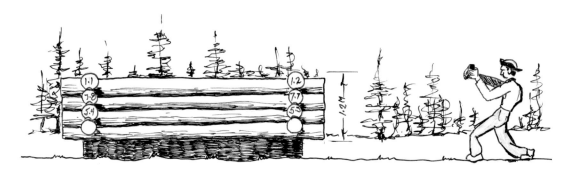

Stand back and judge the level of a wall by sighting across a carpenter's level.

Layout for the Preliminary Notch

Turn the log dogs around to a holding position and secure them so that there is no chance that the log might slip or move. Drive dogs in if you think it is required.

This accomplished, the next step is to scribe the preliminary notches at each end. These notches are to bring the log into the best position for a final scribe, and therefore one notch will most probably be deeper than the other. For this, the log has only to be centered on the wall by eye; you will align the wall with accuracy after the preliminary notches have been cut.

Measure one end on the side of the notch inside the building with the scribers and mark this distance at a convenient location, ideally where the cutting of the scarf will later remove the marks. Measure the other end and mark it in the same place with a common origin (e.g., two concentric arcs). The difference between the two marks will be the difference between the two notches (A & B). Locate a new center (C) about 60 mm from the origin. This will be your final scribe width. Set the scribers from this new mark for each corresponding end. Scribe each notch with the appropriate setting, on both sides of the log at each end of the log (all around the notch).

There are a number of ways to accomplish this same layout. This one is intended to minimize your time and effort. It seems confusing, but go through it step by step until you understand it.

While these are only preliminary notches, not final cuts, it is still a good idea to do a careful scribe, at least in the beginning, until you are practised enough to undertake shortcuts.

Log dogs in a rolling position.

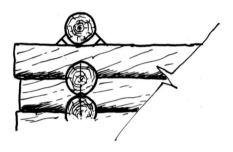

Log dogs in a holding position.

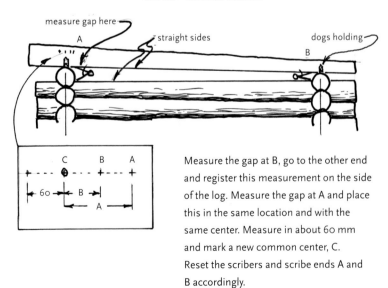

Measure the gap at B, go to the other end and register this measurement on the side of the log. Measure the gap at A and place this in the same location and with the same center. Measure in about 60 mm and mark a new common center, C. Reset the scribers and scribe ends A and B accordingly.

Cutting the preliminary notch for a scarfed log.

to stand on while you do your chopping. If you were so unwise as to roll it outward, you would have less space to stand and you would be in danger of falling off the wall and the log falling on top of you.

CUTTING THE PRELIMINARY NOTCH

The preliminary notch, or as some call it, the rough notch, can most often be chopped with a good axe just as fast as getting a chainsaw up onto the building. This will not hold true for the final cut, but there are other compensations. For this first notch, stand upright with one foot on each wall. Cut a V-notch in the center that starts as close to the scribe line as you can manage. A four-pound Arvika axe with a 700-mm handle would be ideal for this. For smaller logs, a three-pound Oxhead would be quite suitable.

Hold the handle of the axe close to the end in your right hand and lift the axe with your left hand slid partway toward the head. As the swing nears the top, slide your left hand toward the end of the handle until your hands touch, then complete the swing. Practise on the ground on waste wood until you have confidence and accuracy.

After you have removed as much wood as you can from the notch without going over the line, shorten your hold until both hands are close together and about 300 mm from the head of the axe. You can now move in close and chip out the line of the notch to a depth of about 15 mm. Keep the handle above the horizontal and use the nose of the blade to carve with. You can again use a chopping motion to

Remove the dogs on the inside of the log and roll the log inward on the wall until the scribe is upward. Unsightly gouge marks left by the peavey can be avoided if the point is placed carefully into a knot or other depression. Because the bow of the log was outward when you placed the scribe, the bow will have to rotate over the top to the inside in order to have the notch exposed. Be prepared to hold this weight in check and to place a log dog to restrain it if required.

These first notches will be cut with the log up on the building. Because you rolled it inward, you will have the corner of the house

remove the remaining wood from the inside of
the notch, still with the short grip on the tool.
Lastly, carve in a scriber relief at the top of the
notch (see illustration).

scriber relief

Scriber relief allows the
lower leg of the scriber to
go under the log if the
final notch goes above
the midpoint.

ALIGNING THE LOGS

Roll the log back into place and into a rough
alignment. Be careful that the log goes over
without bouncing. Cut the ends off a little
longer than the final length planned, about 50
mm, and snap a chalkline down what you
judge to be the center of the weight of the log,
from end to end. If the log is bowed (to the
outside) the line will be a little closer to the
inside at the middle and closer to the outside at
the ends. The line will, most often, pass over the
center of the log at about the position of the
notches.

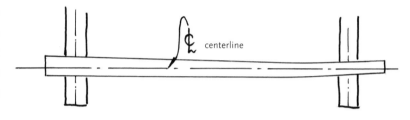

centerline

With the bow of the log to the outside, the centerline will be a
little to the outside at the ends of the log.

Make two marks on each end of the log
plumb with the chalkline: top and bottom
marks. Pinch the log over until these marks are
exactly on the centerline of the wall. Because
this is the first log, there will be no overhang
for reference. An offset reference mark can be
placed on the floor or the adjoining wall about
500 mm from the centerline. With the level, an
identical measurement can be obtained to the
centerline of the current work.

Your work should now be in position for a
final scribe. If the position of the log can be
improved, even a little, it is a good idea to do
so. If the space between the logs is not uniform, this can be changed by lifting one end
or the other with the peavey and sliding a
spacer under the notch. One side can be
blocked up if a few degrees of roll would

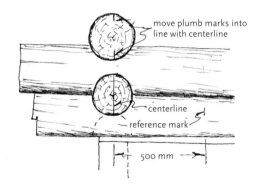

move plumb marks into
line with centerline

centerline

reference mark

500 mm

Centerline of first log
can be located from a
reference mark on the
log below.

make it better, or a notch can be rescribed and recut if such is indicated. At this juncture it pays to be a little fussy.

Scribing

Now your wisdom in obtaining a good pair of scribers will pay dividends. The oldest type of scriber on record appears to have been an iron tool with a selection of two or more fixed claws with which to score parallel marks on the logs. Certainly there must have been other solutions to the problem, but without graphite or ink pencils as we now have, any marking must have been done with a metal point.

My first variation of this tool was an adjustable pair of metal points. This meant the scriber could be more finely adjusted to the log, rather than having to block the log to suit the scriber. By 1974 I had added a two-way level to the handle so that inexperienced people could produce more reliable work. This device worked so well that the same level attachment, added to Starret dividers as scribers, became an industry standard. My own

Student scribing the groove.

design for scribers was originally intended to relieve the high cost of scribers in some countries. With their self-leveling capability, they have gained some popularity.

Whichever type you have, use your scribers to determine the widest gap between the two logs by feeling with the points. Register this span at some handy location. If you have good logs, this setting will be correct for the notches.

Make a second mark a short distance beyond this measurement, usually 5 mm, and this will be the setting for the groove. This is called "overscribing" and it is intended to keep the notches tighter as the logs shrink. Overscribing may vary from inside to outside and from one region to another; however, 5 or 6 mm will work. You might consult with a local log builder for regional practise.

It is a standard practice to start the bottom round with a 12-mm overscribe, then drop 1 mm each round (e.g., 11 mm on the second round, 10 mm on the third, etc.). When you get to the eighth round, where the overscribe will be 5 mm, the groove may be too narrow. In this case, choose a suitable groove width, a scriber setting that will result in a groove width of about 60 to 70 mm, then reduce this setting by 5 mm for the notch. Reduce it 4 mm for the next round and so on.

Take your scribers, with this setting firmly fixed, to the level board. This may simply be a clean board about 300 mm long that is firmly fastened to a solid and handy location. Set the levels carefully so that both bubbles register center while the points are on the line. The quality of your fit will depend, to a large degree, on the accuracy of this setting.

Your scriber should be equipped with an

indelible or ink pencil and the wood can be dampened slightly to obtain a more distinct line. Use a spray bottle or even a damp cloth or sponge. Hold the scriber with both hands and at 45 degrees to the direction of travel. For the notch, start at the top or bottom and go halfway. Then complete from the other direction. Watch only the bubbles while you do this and depend on your sense of feel to make sure the points are contacting. Pay particular attention that the adjusting screws of the scriber do not interfere and leave you with an erroneous line. Do spot checks when you are finished to discover any errors that may have crept in.

When the next logs are scribed it will also be necessary to scribe the overhang or exterior portion of the wall. For this the scribers will be taken back to your reference mark and opened another 5 or 6 mm. This is to prevent "hang-up" at the overhang of the log. Lastly, check all around the scribe to see that no portion has been omitted, then again roll the notches up for cutting and dog it in place.

CUTTING THE FINAL NOTCH

Production yards and individuals who have truck-mounted cranes will lift the log off the building at this point and place it on set blocks on the ground for convenient working. This is an effective practice and has certain obvious advantages. This same technique can be used with a floor hoist, especially if it is equipped with an electric winch. In this case, however, leave the log up on the wall and do the required work there. In the past this was always the way it was done and the skill required is well worth practising.

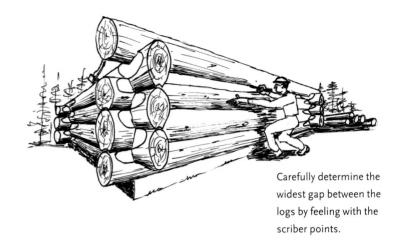

Carefully determine the widest gap between the logs by feeling with the scriber points.

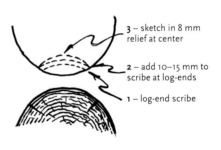

3 – sketch in 8 mm relief at center

2 – add 10–15 mm to scribe at log-ends

1 – log-end scribe

close-fitted log will hang up and lift

The lower line represents the groove scribe and need not be drawn on the log end. The next line up is overscribed 10 to 15 mm and should be drawn on the log. Another 5 mm is added in the center. This will be the cutting line.

Overscribing the log-end portion (overhang) should prevent hang-up when the log checks.

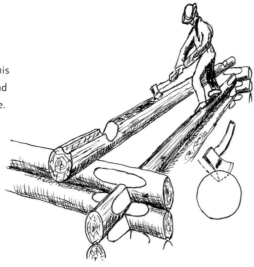

Notches and grooves can be cut on the building with an axe. This requires skill, energy and a good sense of balance.

a reasonably smooth cut that is a few millimeters low in the center. The groove can first be scored with the axe (see illustration) and finished with the axe, a scorp or a heavy gouge chisel (a shovel gouge).

With practise, this work can be accomplished with surprising speed and accuracy. When I was building the house at the Silloep Hill ranch, I would put as many as ten logs a day on the building by these means. They were long days, indeed, but the satisfaction was immense and it was what I wanted to do. It was an experience I would not trade away and I hope, at whatever speed you progress, your satisfaction is at least as great.

The final notches are cut exactly the same way that the preliminary or rough notch was cut, except that you might score just inside the scribe line with the chisel first. Leave the line on and score at right angles to the log to a depth of about 5 mm. If at first you are nervous about working too close to the line with the axe, stay 10 or 12 mm back and finish to the line with your chisels. You should end up with

TREATING AND INSULATING THE NOTCH

Your log may now be replaced in the location it is to occupy for the next two hundred years. If you are totally confident of your workmanship, the groove and notches can be treated and insulated before the log is turned down. However, for the first few rounds it might be more realistic to try the log in place first. It is best if there are no adjustments needed. Making small corrections because the scribe or the cutting was not accurate can be both time consuming and frustrating. After a little practise, they will not be necessary.

Your log will fit, but as you try it in place, take advantage of the opportunity to drill holes for electrical, plumbing or openings. Drill these holes through the log with a 50-mm auger. Drill into the log below far enough to leave a good mark so that the hole can be extended when this piece is off to be insulated

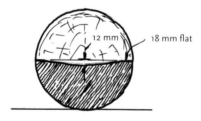

Cross-section through notch.

12 mm   18 mm flat

A heavy slick or shovel gouge can be used to clean out the groove. These must be very sharp. Swallow-tail slick (top) and shovel gouge (bottom).

(see illustration). Mark the location of the drill hole on the side of the log and note the setback so that the next log can be drilled to match.

Again roll the log up and now paint the cut surfaces with a preservative, or better yet, use an emulsified wax sealer as well. Fix and staple fiberglass insulation into the groove and notch. Use as much as you think you can get in without holding the log up with it. This will, for most purposes, make a satisfactory seam. Even more effective, and almost mandatory if driven rain is a problem, is a strip of EM SEAL on each side of the groove and notch. This is a tar-impregnated foam strip that comes in a variety of sizes and does a first-rate job. In addition, use the fiberglass as before. All that now remains to do is to cut the scarf. Lay out the scarf with the template or scarf board and cut the scarf the same as you did on the first logs.

Congratulations! Your first full hand-fitted log is complete.

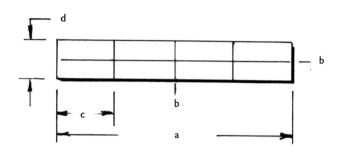

A scarf board can be made from light plywood or plastic. The size is dictated by the size of your logs. This template is used to obtain better uniformity of the scarf.
a) length of flat
b) centerlines
c) length of cove
d) width of groove (next log)

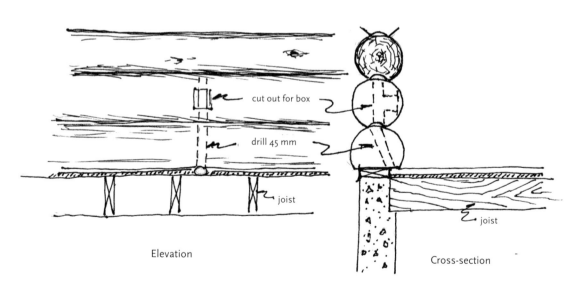

Elevation

Cross-section

Place holes for electrical wires as the walls are built. For offsite building, these are best done as the walls are disassembled.

Chapter 9

Log Walls

As the walls go up, you can expect a number of situations to develop that will challenge your experience and imagination. The first of these has to do with wall height. If the building is the same as Plan 793 of *Log House Plans*, with just four walls to contend with, this should not be any problem. If the plan is more complex, it is even more important to measure the height of each log at the corner and mark this height on the log-end. The height of even-numbered logs should not vary by more than 30 mm. If they do, you should make every effort in your log selection to correct this (see Log Selection, Chapter 8).

Lock Notch

Let's say the top end of a log is too small to cover an outsized butt end and leave enough wood for adequate strength. Nevertheless it is the right-sized log to maintain the wall height. In this situation you will have to employ another variation of the saddle notch,

one that has become known as a "lock notch."

This notch will be scribed in the same way as the saddle notch with a little additional layout. When the regular scribe has been completed (Step 1), draw a level line across the notch at a height that will leave sufficient

Every builder must be familiar with and able to lay out and cut a lock notch properly. If the saddle notch extends more than halfway through the upper log, you should use a lock notch.

Step 1 – Normal scribe.

Step 2 – Place level lines across the scribe (a–a). Drop points to the lower log (c–c). These will be the same scribe setting and originate at the intersection of the scribe line and the level line.

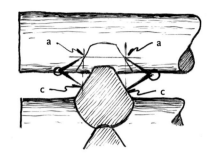

Step 3 – Cut the notch to the level line, then measure in 15–30 mm from points a–a and cut the top half of the notch.

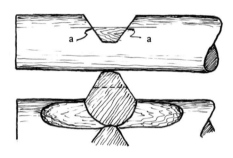

Step 4 – Measure in from points c–c the same as the upper log (15–30 mm) and cut receiver. Cut the flat 3 mm low for clearance.

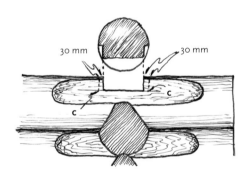

wood in the notch for strength. Drop two scribe points on each side of the notch to the log below (Step 2). These marks should be placed with a high degree of accuracy. The scribers will still be set to the original scribe distance. The marks you are placing must be precisely below the intersection of the original notch scribe where the level line intersects it. The rest of the layout is done after the log has been rolled up.

Join corresponding pairs of marks with another level line (Step 3). Measure in on this line a suitable distance (usually 30 mm) and join these pairs across the top of the log. This will be your cutout or receiver for the piece left in the notch, to improve the notch strength. The notch is cut in the usual way but only down to the level line. When that has been done, measure in the same distance as above (30 mm) and draw in the lines that will dimension the support block (Step 4). Cut the small segment out to the top of the notch and you are complete.

A better way to do this is to cut a 30-degree slope on both the block and the receiver. Use an adjustable template, as in the illustration, to control the angle and size. Your work will have to be more accurate, but it will provide a better fit as the wood shrinks later on.

Cutting a saddle notch in hemlock logs for Knotingham with a Hytest Australian axe.

RECURVE

Another situation that sometimes comes up is recurve at the scarf. If the scarf was not cut deeply enough for the particular log selected, the scarf will have to be extended to avoid a recurved notch. This can easily be determined after the final scribe setting has been fixed. Try your scriber at each of the four corners of the notch. If the lower point goes below the scarf a short distance, you should be able to cut the small corner of the scarf a little deeper with a slick or chisel. If the scribe goes a long way past the scarf, there is something wrong. Either the new log is too large or too crooked, in which case the bottom of the new log might be hewn down in order to remove some of the bend, or another log altogether will have to be chosen.

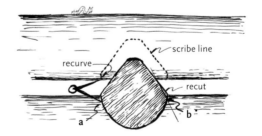

Check all four corners of the notch for recurve, which is when the scribe goes below the scarf (a). Recut the scarf if required (b).

GROOVES

There are several kinds of lengthwise groove shapes, but when you are working without a chainsaw, you are almost limited to a round, cove (concave) shape. This is not a great concern since I feel that this is the best shape for the groove. For special purposes you might want to use other profiles and for that reason they will be described here. Realistically, they will have to be cut with a chainsaw.

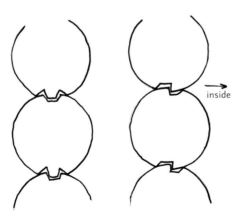

Locking groove for weather seal.

Z-groove to retain upper log in place.

inside

The first is a locking groove to improve weather tightness. The second is for the upper rounds of a building to prevent any displacement of the upper log. For the first, you will have to do a double scribe on the groove. Place a scribe line on both the upper and lower logs. When the upper log has been rolled, two grooves are cut along each scribe line to a depth of about 25 mm, which will leave a ridge in the center. A single, shallow trench is cut into the lower log starting a short way inside the scribe line (e.g., 20 mm). Use the scribe line as a guide. This groove provides a good secure location for a seal such as EM.

For the second locking groove, a double scribe is needed only on the inside, while the outside is scribed in the usual way. When the upper log has been rolled, place a center chalkline in corresponding positions on each log. Cut this line to a depth of about 30 mm with a chainsaw cut centered on the line. Complete the groove on the outside half of the upper log and the inside half of the lower log. This groove is used on the upper two rounds of your house because there is less weight on these logs. The groove might open if these top logs dry too quickly.

FITTING THE OVERHANG

When you reach the second half of the second round, you will start fitting the overhang portion of the wall. To do this, go back to your scribe reference mark and add 5 or 6 mm to the scriber width. Scribe the length of the overhang and also the end of the log. To the end scribe, sketch in an additional 6 mm in the center. The reason for adding this relief on the overhang is that the interior portion of the log may dry more quickly, causing the wall to hang up on the outside piece and loosen the notches. Also, and of greater importance, the log-ends often check in the center and spread. If there is no clearance, this may cause the end of the log to touch or "hang up" on the log below.

ELECTRICAL INSTALLATION

Because the logwork for this house is being built in place on the foundation, it will be necessary to provide for electrical wiring installation as you build. This requires that the wiring plan be as complete as possible. If you were building off the foundation, electrical outlets and other installations could be marked on the completed building and drilled into the walls as the structure is being disassembled. But you will install the wire or provide a place for the wire as you go along.

The plan calls for a solid concrete floor, but the finished floor is on wood sleepers and the electrical wires are distributed around the perimeter behind the base trim. This is quite easy and the only thing to watch for is access when the location of the electrical service has been decided upon. Most of the wall outlets will be about 300 mm from the floor, so only the first two or possibly three logs will need to be drilled. In some instances it will be required

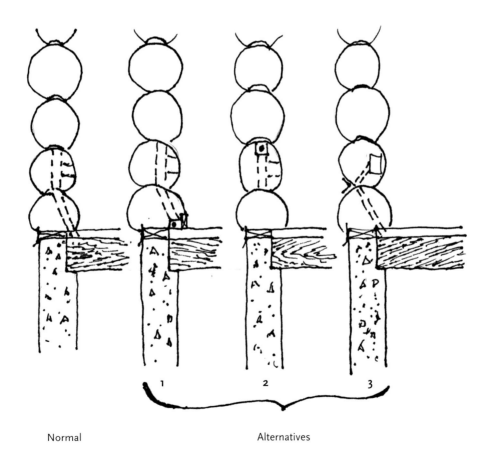

Normal   Alternatives

Normal electrical access is from under the floor. Alternative placement:
1) behind the baseboard
2) along the groove
3) zigzagged up the wall.

to go higher and this is described in Chapter 15. When the height for the wall outlet has been reached, drill a smaller hole into the vertical drill hole for the wire to go through. It is a good idea to cut out the mortise for the electrical box at this time and either place a strong cord in the hole (which can be used to pull the wire through later) or else install the wire immediately. If, for instance, the electrical service were installed in the closet near the kitchen entrance, wires for the second floor might be placed behind the keyway of the door and drilled on up to the second floor locations (see illustration).

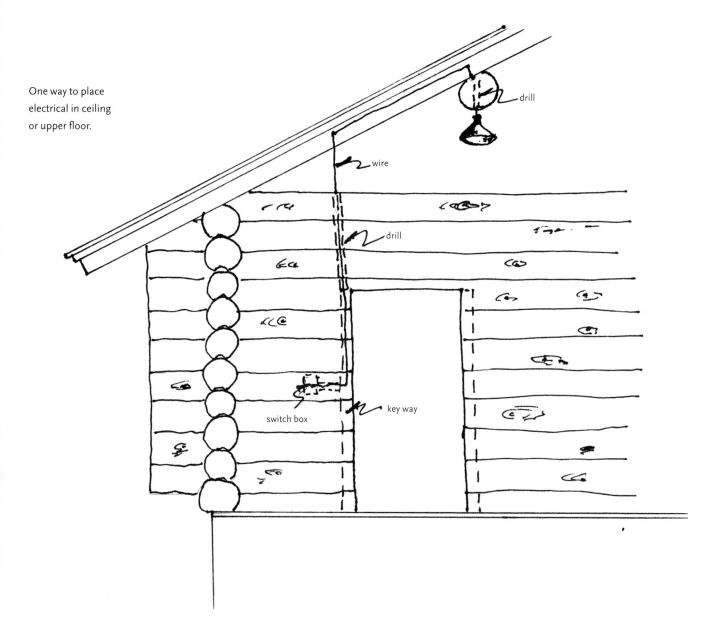

One way to place electrical in ceiling or upper floor.

drill

wire

drill

switch box

key way

Window and Door Openings

Build in window and door openings as you build up the walls. For some people, this seems a little awkward, but there are good reasons to learn how to do this. First, you can save a great deal of material by using short pieces from crooked logs. Second, you can keep the wall line true and vertical, and this is especially important at the doors and windows, where a uniform appearance is helpful. Extra care must be used in handling the short logs because they are sitting safely on the wall at only one end. The floor hoist, if it is used, is very handy to hold up the other end.

A great many devices have been developed to try to solve the problem encountered in rolling the short log after the preliminary notch has been scribed. When you are experienced, it is often possible to cut this notch before the log is placed onto the wall and then the need to roll the log is avoided. A cage made of three short pieces of lumber is often used. A more sophisticated version made of square steel tube might also be used if you expect to do a lot of this. Adjustable chalks can be made and a box of slim wood wedges is always handy.

Once the correct scribe location has been obtained, place dogs across the end of the log to avoid any movement. The most common reason for failure with short logs is that, unknown to the builder, the log moved a little during the scribing operation. If possible, remove the short logs from the building for final cutting. If this is not possible, use a scaffold or some other framed support for the free end.

Logs that are in short sections and have only one notch or no notches at all should be pegged. This is done either with wood dowels

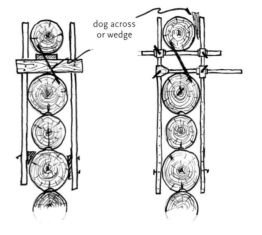

dog across or wedge

Short logs can be controled with a cage made of 2 x 4s or square steel tube.

2 x 4 cage   Adjustable steel cage

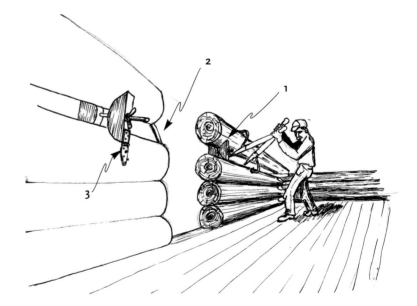

1) Roll logs with great care if you are using adjustable blocks.
2) Use drive dogs across the ends to secure log in position.
3) Strap-hinges on the block, screwed to the lower log, will improve stability.

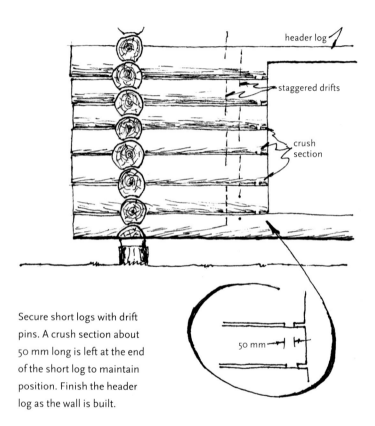

header log

staggered drifts

crush
section

50 mm

Secure short logs with drift
pins. A crush section about
50 mm long is left at the end
of the short log to maintain
position. Finish the header
log as the wall is built.

or with short metal drift pins. For wood dowels, use material that is about 38 mm in diameter and stagger the drill holes. Mark the location of these holes on the side of the log for reference. For steel, drill only the top log and a short distance into the lower log, then drive them down the rest of the way. Continue building the wall in this manner until you have reached the top of the windows.

Another useful trick with short logs is to leave a "crush" section at the end. Obviously, if you are overscribing the groove 5 mm, 6 mm or more, the overscribe will accumulate and the logs will tend to sag at the opening. In the past we overcame this by adding a wedge at the end of each log. A crush piece is a short portion at the end of the log that has been scribed with the same scriber setting as the notch, perhaps for a distance of 150 mm. This will be sufficient to hold the log in place but it will crush down and not hinder the settling of the building.

The log across the top of the windows will be called the "header" log and will be at a height of about 2100 mm above the floor. A little variation is permissible to allow the top cut of the window to be made just below the midpoint of the header log. While this header log is being scribed, lay out the top cut for the window or doorway. Measure the 2100 mm height from the floor, add the scribe distance and place a mark at this point on each side of the window. Snap a chalkline between these marks and repeat the process on the other side of the log. Mark the centerline of the window on the underside of the log so that the ends of the flat can be located after the log has been turned over.

Now, while the header log is being shaped for placement on the wall, the top side of the window or door space can also be cut. As you may well guess, it is very much easier to do a good job of this cut in the working position rather than trying to work upside down when the log is in place. It is also important to start the cut for the keyway (the groove in the log ends in which the keypiece for the window or door will fit) while the work is in this position. For our purpose, let's consider the key stock (the material used to fit into the keyway to prevent displacement) to be 40 mm x 90 mm. This mortise is almost always made with a chainsaw, and that is the main reason for starting the cut now. When the log is in place, it can be dangerous to make this cut because kickback of the chainsaw is very possible. I have often made this cut with hand tools by drilling an auger hole at the back of the cut, and then removing the wood with a chisel. If you wish to make the keyway by hand all the way up the sides of the windows and doors, you will have to locate the opening with some accuracy right at the start and place the drill holes as each log is completed.

SETTLING

You are now close to the top of the walls, which should finish high enough that they will not be too low when the building has completed settling. Settling is one aspect of log buildings that must be kept in mind at all times. Walls, windows, doors, roof structures, stairways, fireplaces and furniture are all affected by settling. This is not a problem since we have devised ways to deal with the settling of each of these parts of the house. It just has to be kept in mind.

The settling rate for green logs is about 1:16 (1 mm for every 16 mm of wood). If you wish to have the undersides of the floor joists at a final height of 2400 mm, they will have to be built to a height of 2560 mm. If the floor joists have an average diameter of 200 mm and you want them to notch halfway into the log that will carry them, then the top of the wall log should be near 2660 mm. Try to bring the walls to this same height at each corner, but if there is a little difference it is not in any way a problem.

Settling at doors and windows is treated the same way. If a window is to be 1600 mm high, then it could settle 100 mm and the opening should be 1700 mm. You need only be concerned with the height of logs within the opening itself. The same applies to each location that can be expected to settle.

Floor Joists

The top rounds of logs will use lock notches. Outriggers and floor joists should be placed with square notches or, as they are sometimes called, double-scribe notches. This is done to give them a good appearance from the underside even if they are not the best fit, although by this time that will not be a problem. The important reason for using this notch is so that the log can be notched down halfway while removing very little of the height of its diameter.

Log floor-joists can be flattened on one side in the same way that you flattened the first logs when you were starting to build the walls. It is not required to have a great wide flat on the log; the very least you can get a line on is ample. These can be sawn accurately with a chainsaw mill, but we will again work by hand and do it with the broadaxe.

Mark the centerline location for each floor joist on the top wall log, then position the floor joists across the building on these marks. The flat side, which you have just hewn, will, of course, be facing up. Sometimes the joists will be alternated top to butt. Because each log will be of a somewhat different size, it will be necessary to find a way to bring all the flat-top sides into alignment. Be careful that the flat is level across and that the log is well dogged so that it will not move.

Because the top of the floor joist is intended to reach 2760 mm, measure the actual height above the floor and subtract the difference. This difference will be the scriber setting. For example, if the measured height is 2870 mm, the scriber setting will be 110 mm. Each end of the log should have the same scriber setting. If they differ, the low end should be blocked up or the high end rough-notched down to make them equal. Put two pencils into your scriber so that a double scribe can be accomplished in one operation. Set your scriber distance and set the levels with great care at the level board. This scribe is done in one operation and often the scribe distance is wider than ordinarily would be the case, so a little extra care would be in order.

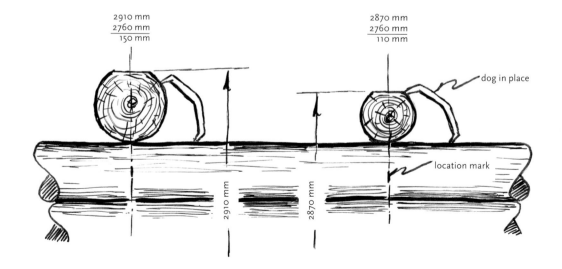

Calculate the scribe setting by subtracting your target height from the actual height (height above the floor).

Scribe each end of the joist and be sure that the two lines are complete before you move the log (Step 1). Draw a level line across the notch that will divide the scribe height (Step 2). The higher you place the level line, the more strength you will cut out of the floor joist. But if you place it too low, the notch will be difficult to cut. Use your judgment and make a reasonable compromise. With the same scriber setting, find the point of intersection from this level line to the scribe line below. From this point, bring another level line across the lower scribe. Again use the scribers to find the point on the upper scribe and place a level line there. Drop the last point down from the end of this line and your layout is complete. Do both notches and you can roll the log over. Use a tape or a flexible straight-edge to join the ends of the level line across the top of the log (Step 3) and then the flat part of the notch is ready to cut.

Saw the edges down and dress out (clean up) the flat portion on each log. Score the top half of each notch and remove this segment with the chisel. The joist should now roll back into place at the correct height. Repeat the same procedure on each joist and they should all be in alignment and at the right height.

PLATE LOGS AND CAP LOGS

The house plan you are using goes up another 2100 mm to the plate log (the last log on the wall, from which the roofline will originate) to provide an upper floor area. In some localities this is not allowed because of seismic considerations. In order to obtain a comparable floor area and stay within the regulations, you will

Step 1 – A double-scribe notch or square notch is scribed with two pencils in the scriber.

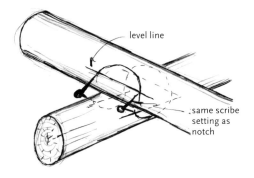

Step 2 – Lay out level lines on both of the logs. These will be the scribe distance apart.

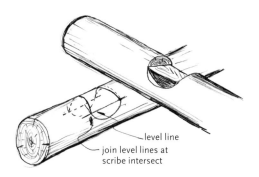

Step 3 – Cut the flat to the level line first. The coved portion should be moved in at least 15 mm top and bottom. Be careful! This requires a slightly different cut on each log.

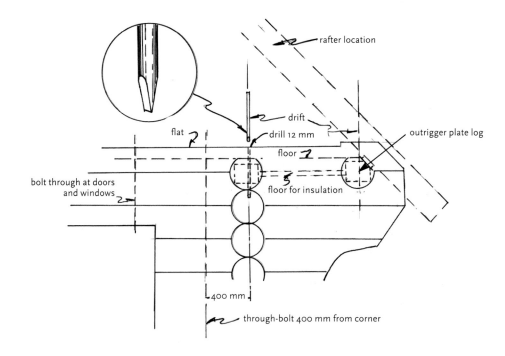

Roof height can be increased by using an outrigger plate (generally 600–750 mm). Drift the top two or three rounds together.

rafter location

drift

flat

drill 12 mm

outrigger plate log

floor

bolt through at doors and windows

floor for insulation

400 mm

through-bolt 400 mm from corner

need to use an outrigger purlin and a steeper roof. The outrigger should be positioned at the same level as the floor joists and secured with square notches.

The next logs to go on the wall will be the cap logs, which will cover the ends of the floor joists and, if applicable, the outrigger. With this modification, the walls of your house are up. The only jobs outstanding are to trim and sand the log-ends, if this has not already been done as you go (see Chapter 14 for log-end treatment) and to pin the top two rounds together with drift pins.

A drift pin is a smooth steel pin with a chisel point, 12 mm in diameter and about 300 mm to 400 mm long. Drill through the top log with a 12-mm drill and grease the pin before it is driven. Drive it, with the chisel point across the grain, down 12 mm to 18 mm below the surface of the plate log.

THE SATISFACTION OF A JOB WELL DONE

Your walls are now complete and you can take a few days to stand back and visit with them. I like to go back to the work site in the evening and just sit and look at the work and feel the satisfaction of a job well done. There are no large gaps from an overcut notch, there are no scarfs that have been cut too deeply and the log-ends show a uniform pattern without any overcut grooves to disturb the symmetry. I know this already, but I look again anyway just to feel the pleasure of knowing that I have treated the logs with the greatest respect that I can. I also like to look again to see if there is anything I can improve upon the next time. For me, building log houses is a little bit like eating chocolates: one is never enough and the next one might be better.

*Mr. Kim and I brushing one of
the floor joists flat to the line.*

Mr. Kim, the Director of the B. Allan Mackie School of Log Building in Korea, came to help me put the house up. Until I met the Korean people, I thought that New Zealanders were the nicest people on earth. In my thirty years of teaching and building log buildings, I have met many kind, generous and happy people, and the Koreans have to be among the greatest of these.

Mr. Kim came to Toronto. I picked him up at the airport and we went out to Shanty Lake. I worked him very hard for two weeks. He was a long way from his friends and Korean food, sleeping in a tent and plagued by mosquitoes and rain. Yet he was cheerful and happy the whole time.

The site chosen for the building was a higher rock outcrop across a wet patch from the log pile. We cut up a lot of the poles and brush that had been produced by site clearing and we corduroyed the road. This is the process of laying logs close by each other across the road then covering it all with about 30 cm of earth.

I was able to position the building so that two of the corners would be on solid rock. They are big rocks, possibly the size of Australia, so I have

Sill logs under Knotingham. The log post was later replaced with rockwork.

little concern about them being moved by frost. I picked two other rocks, a little smaller, and moved them into position for the other two corners. They ended up surprisingly near level.

We flattened four large pine logs top and bottom for foundation beams. I made them flat on the bottom in case I want to build a complete rock foundation at some future date. Mr. Kim and I placed these on the rocks and lap-notched them together. At this time we were still able to carry the logs across with the backhoe. As we came to the re-erection of the building, it became necessary to chain the logs to the blade of a small dozer and walk them across the small swampy place.

The foundation logs were in place and the floor joists were cut in according to the blueprint, but we needed flooring, insulation and plywood to compete the floor. I had made arrangements with a nearby builder to supply these materials so all we had to do was transport them in. I trucked the material as near as possible then off-loaded it to the log trailer and towed it in behind the crawler tractor.

Fortunately the Toronto crew was available for another work bee and we put the walls up. Again, the first half-logs were selected and moved to the foundation. We put EM SEAL on the bottom flat surface and between the logs as we went up. I can't help sounding like a paid advertisement for EM SEAL. This sealing material is absolutely superb and I have to recommend it for any log or timber building. It will save its cost many times over in fuel economy and it's worth its weight in comfort.

That said, it is also of the greatest importance to build carefully. It is a temptation to rush the building up with as much noise and confusion as possible. But later, especially when you are a long way off the road and the nights are long and cold, you will proud of your draft-free, mouse-proof building. Mice are friendly little critters way out here and see no reason why they should not share your accommodation. They do tend to get into things and make a lot of noise at night but it is a shame to kill them just because they are so naive. Better to make a mouse-proof building.

The second day was long and hard. Now the walls were higher and we had to be extremely careful. A fall or other injury could be very serious this far from the road. Accidents are directly proportional to your willingness to take a chance. We took no chances.

Mr. Kim did so much want to put the roof on the building but time did not allow. He was, however, able to make up the ridge log from a large, straight white pine log. He forgot to sign it so I will have him remedy that the next time he comes.

By the time Mr. Kim left, the walls for Knotingham were completely finished.

CHAPTER 10

NOTCHES OF ALL KINDS

THE QUALITIES OF A GOOD NOTCH

All of the notches that have been invented can be made with hand tools. Some of the more complicated ones can be slow to shape, but with skill comes satisfaction. Each notch, simple or complicated, provides satisfaction for the builder. Speed is a thrill for contractors and developers.

I have already described the most common construction notches: the saddle notch, lock notch and double-scribed notch. Without getting into the mortise and tenon notches that more properly belong to timber framing and roof structures, there are still a few good types that can be most useful for wall construction.

To be classified as a good notch, the design must possess certain qualities desirable to the builder. The notch should be water-resistant (a shape that tends to repel water), wind-resistant (a shape that seals easily and tightly); roll-resistant and self-locking (the logs remain in place). The notch should also have a good appearance, with a design that suits the style of the building. The notch should be strong, because it is possible to design a notch that cuts away too much of the wood and leaves another part of the log too frail. And lastly, the notch should be simple. You can use a complex join where it has a use, but complexity for its own sake is a form of snobbery.

The notches you have already used fit these criteria. The saddle notch resists weather, is simple and quick to cut, easy to seal and roll-resistant. It does not lock well in place but the next log will provide that security. If, because of difficult log selection, a saddle notch is too weak, you can resort to a lock notch, which will provide the strength and also, if required, the locking aspect. Double-scribed notches retain water in the lower portion if they are exposed, so these are not desirable on most wall locations. They can provide a better appearance in some applications and they are very good for strength and roll resistance.

Round Notch

Round notches enjoy little popularity within the log-building industry. This is understandable in that round notches require greater skill to work the logs and a more uniform log supply than is easily available. I think that the round notch is the most natural-looking notch to use on round-log construction, but I am forced to agree that there are real hazards in its use, particularly if the logs are not straight and well matched. The problem lies with the shrinkage of the logs. Even if the logs are well seasoned before use, there will still be an appreciable shrinkage after construction. As the lower log shrinks in diameter, the notch remains the same size and even an excellent fit will loosen. This is especially true if the notch goes beyond the diameter line of the lower log. I leave it to your judgment to decide if this notch is for you. (See Chapter 8.)

Finishing a round notch on Ardea.

Dovetail corner in round logs.

DOVETAIL NOTCH

Traditional dovetail cornering is a very good and useful notch that meets all the criteria I have identified. It is water-resistant, weather-tight, simple, neat and stable. It is unacceptable to some building authorities for structural applications on the grounds that is not self-locking and therefore unstable in areas subject to seismic activity. Nevertheless, this notch has been around for a very long time and has performed well. One story tells of a Russian-built log house in Alaska with dovetail corners that was swept several hundreds of meters up a mountainside by a tidal wave and left on a rakish angle. The house is still intact today. In any case, the corner is useful in non-load-bearing situations where it would be awkward to have protruding log-ends. If this notch is used on round-log construction, it will be necessary to flatten both sides of the log for at least a short distance back.

Each log used should be cut to the same width (e.g., 175 mm). Place the bottom log at the desired angle (this need not be 90 degrees) and fix or dog it very firmly with the flattened sides vertical and plumb. Draw vertical lines at each of the four corners of the notch. Locate a level line around the log-end at the vertical midpoint. The level line may be just a tick at each of the four vertical lines. The inside corner and the diagonal outside corner will be the same height. The corner across the log from the inside corner will be 15 mm lower than the level mark and the fourth corner will be 15 mm higher. Draw in the lines and cut the notch. If the center of the flat is a little low (1 mm), the fit may be better.

Place the next log on top of this one, dog it

Layout for a dovetail.

1) level line at half log height
2) 15 mm up at width of log
3) level line from extended cut line
4) 15 mm up for cut line
5) level line from cut line
6) 15 mm down – extend cut line to back

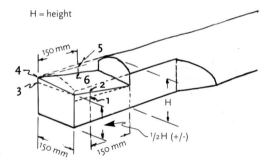

H = height

First half-log

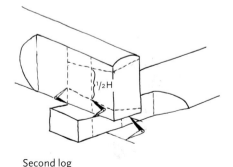

Second log

in place, then set your scribers in the usual way (to the widest gap between the logs plus the overscribe (See Chapter Eight). Scribe and cut this log and you are ready to repeat the cycle. It is a good idea to build in a short temporary overhang on each of the logs to keep them in position while you build. This overhang should be removed upon completion because it may retain water. A properly proportioned dovetail is very stable and tends to become tighter as the log dries.

Another style of this notch is a locking dovetail, which resists displacement (see illustration). Another is the blind dovetail notch, which you used on the very first round of logs (see Chapter 8).

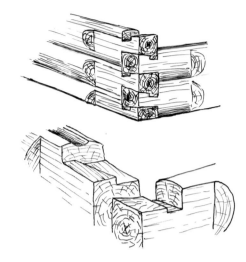

Locking dovetail.

Sill logs for piece-on-piece construction, with a locking dovetail corner.

Blind Wall Dovetail Notch

There is another useful blind dovetail that can be used in wall construction where you do not wish to have an intersecting wall to show on the other side. Place your log in the usual manner but use only a very minimal rough notch. Overhang is not required, since the log is trimmed to the centerline of the one below

Layout for a blind dovetail wall notch.

FIGURE 1

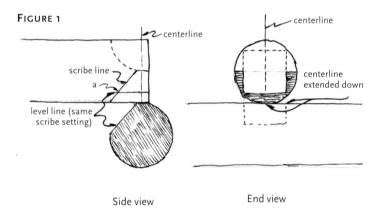

centerline

scribe line

a

level line (same scribe setting)

centerline

centerline extended down

Side view   End view

FIGURE 2

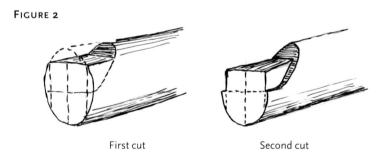

First cut   Second cut

before the final scribe is applied. Double-scribe the notch and place a level line on your new log that will represent the bottom of the dovetail. Use the scribe setting to locate this distance on the lower scribe line and repeat the layout on the other side of the log.

Before this log is moved for cutting, draw a vertical centerline on the end and extend it to the log below. Also draw the outside corners of the dovetail and extend these to the log below (see Fig. 1). You now have the reference marks needed to finish the layout when the log is rolled.

When the log has been turned up, cut the notch in the usual way, only as deep as the level line. Relocate the centerline on this newly formed flat surface. Measure out from the back end of this centerline a distance 10 mm less than the front corners of the dovetail (to form a dovetail shape) (see Fig. 2). Cut straight down and remove this segment of wood. On the lower log, draw the level line across the two reference marks, duplicate the measurements from the upper log and cut out the mortise. Make this a good tight fit to hold the half-notch firmly in place.

When the time comes to add another log on the top, follow much the same procedure. The important part of the layout is to transfer the location of the centerlines from one log to the other with accuracy so that the work can be referenced to these marks.

SHEEP'S HEAD NOTCH

If you have the inclination to use an exotic notch, you might choose to do the whole building with sheep's head notches. To do this, start with the lower log scarfed with a long scarf. Place your new log with a small rough notch and determine a scribe distance. In this layout you will be using a scarf on the bottom half of the notch as well as a double scarf on the upper portion.

Mark your scribe distance on the side of the new log and use this mark as the top of the lower scarf. Roll the log over and cut this scarf, then replace the log for the final scribe. When the scribe has been completed, place a level line on each side of the notch at a point halfway between the top of the lower log and the top of the scribe. From where this level line intersects the scribe line, use the same scriber setting and drop 4 points onto the lower log. From the top of the notch at the centerline, place a plumb mark on the lower log that will provide a reference for the width and location of the notch. Roll the log. Measure in 30 mm from the last reference mark on the lower log and cut to the level line at a 30-degree slope. Cut the upper log in the usual way only to the level line. Transfer measurements from the lower notch and finish the sides of the notch on the upper log. Cut the other half of the scarf and the notch is done.

With the exception of the timber-framing notches, which will be discussed in Chapter 11, these examples will give you enough variation to meet any need. A good building can be built using only a saddle notch. A better building will use some of these other refinements.

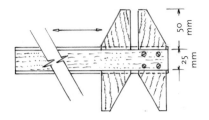

An adjustable template can be used to find the angle.

Sheeps' head notch: very much like a lock notch with sloped sides.

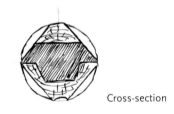

Cross-section

Sheeps' head notch.

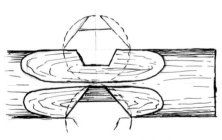

Side view

CHAPTER 11

DIFFERENT WALLS FOR DIFFERENT HALLS

When I was growing up, I was more interested in the woods and the wild creatures than I was in urban life. Fortunately we lived in the country and had many books. Through those books, I learned about birds (I knew them all by name), trees (I could recognize all the kinds we had), hunting and woodcraft.

But the things that I learned that have been the greatest comfort to me, I learned without even realizing it. Now I still know the sounds of summer, the feel of autumn and spring, the smell of an approaching storm and a thousand other things that tell me what nature is feeling and doing.

Many people growing up now will never know these things and I wonder if the sterilized life we live will provide the same satisfaction in days to come. I hope so. Perhaps it will, but for me, the fond memories are found in the peace in the woods and the peaceful quiet of a log house.

MY FIRST LOG HOUSE

The first log house that I can remember was of piece-on-piece construction. I remember this building as a stable used for the big, patient horses only at the exciting time of harvest, when there was no time for them to be taken home to be fed. We ate our sandwiches with the dusty men in the shade of the great logs. It was a cool, dark building that stood among the sweeping willows and rustling poplars that bordered the grain fields.

Later I learned that this building had a much more substantial history. It had been built as a trading station a little less than a hundred years before by the fur traders of the North West Company. In 1903 it was purchased by my grandfather and moved to the nearby pioneer town of Battleford to be used as a general store. In 1916 it was again moved, in one piece, fifteen miles to the west and was enlarged by my father to use his first house. It was moved twice more to

Piece-on-piece building with frame in place and infill logs being positioned.

ADVANTAGES OF PIECE-ON-PIECE

This style of building was particularly suited for an area where trees were plentiful and big but not very long. Using this system, it was possible to build a house or other building to almost any size with short logs. Short logs had other advantages as well: they were easily transported and easily moved onto the building. These logs were hewn flat on the inside and the outside and the sills, uprights and headers were hewn on all four sides.

There were several good reasons why this seemingly extra work was undertaken. First, it made the logs lighter and easier to lift. Second, it gave the building a more ordered look, and order, rightly or wrongly, was one of the things that people felt they needed to impose on this vast and intimidating new land. Third, the flat sides were better aligned and this provided a surface that could be stripped and plastered, either with mud or stucco, depending on the builder's ability. This treatment was often necessary because the logs were not scribed together and there was little by way of efficient caulking or chinking material available. Another reason for stucco or plaster was that the log panels would shrink and fall away from the top plate and leave a large space for wind and snow and dust to infiltrate. Now there are tools and techniques to overcome these problems so that if you choose to, you can still benefit from the advantages of short-log buildings.

its final location, and has now sunk into the fertile soil of the prairie. This building was piece-on-piece. The logs were big, and I remember almost every log, because so much of my childhood was spent crawling over it or playing hide-and-seek around and about it. The axe marks, the grooves and the tenons I can still see in my mind. The logs were poplar and a silver-gray in color.

Traditional piece-on-piece or post-in-the-sill construction.

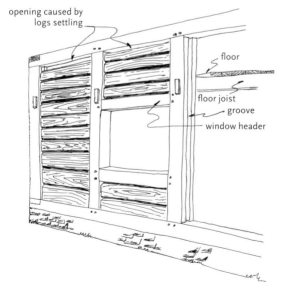

opening caused by logs settling

floor

floor joist

groove

window header

DEVELOPMENT OF PIECE-ON-PIECE

In choosing a system of building, it is always important to me to consider not only the technical advantage of the system but also to remain faithful to the traditional background of the style. A good design will include these factors and with this in mind, I would like to look at the traditional style of piece-on-piece and then at some of the other designs for this style of building.

It used to be called post-in-the-sill, but is now more often referred to as piece-on-piece.

This building style was transported to Canada from Normandy, France, where it had been developed and used for much the same reasons considered above. Originally, it was called *colombage* and the panels or infill was of rubble rock, not wood. When the system was brought to Canada, logs were used because of their abundance and their greater insulating properties. In time, the French-Canadian axemen became very proficient at putting up these buildings and they built strong, stout, long-lasting structures, many of which are still in existence today. Unfortunately, the first log building I remember had no foundation, and for this reason is no longer standing.

PREPARING THE LOGS

To build such a building, the first requirement is to obtain good-sized material. A favorite size for posts and framing was 280 mm (11 inches) square. To produce such a piece of timber, you would need a log 395 mm on the top end. However, it would not be essential to have the post totally squared out and a little waney edge (an edge that has not been milled) would be all right. Nevertheless, it would still require a good log to do a building to this standard.

When the plates and posts have been hewn square, they can be fitted together with standard timber-framing techniques. Some people use sawn timbers for this, but rough-sawn timber presents a very inferior appearance. If you use this kind of material, you might need to plane carefully.

Most framers work from a face edge, using two adjacent sides of each timber for a base for measurements. This is good practise if the timbers have been sized with a planer, but hewn timbers may vary more in dimension. I have found it better to work from a centerline originally imposed on each end when the timber is first laid out. Another thing that I have found helpful is to make the timbers slightly oversize (by about 5 mm). This will allow for inaccuracy or remanufacture if needed.

From the centerlines and chalklines, lay out and cut the length and the tenons and mortises

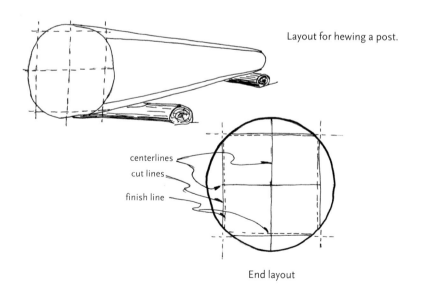

Layout for hewing a post.

centerlines

cut lines

finish line

End layout

an electric dado saw. I use a special electric saw equipped with a cutter head and various sizes. It does a nice job. Neither the posts nor, for that matter, any other part of the building need be left in an unfinished state. You can plane the inside of the posts and then carve panels or embellish the edge to whatever degree your time or taste indicates.

In the traditional building, the infill logs had a short tenon cut onto the end. More often we now use a dado on each part and a spline to retain the panel logs. The plate logs at the top and the sill logs at the bottom can be lap-notched together. Ideally the sill and plate logs would be full-length pieces but if not, they can be spliced or the plan of the building geared to suit shorter lengths.

Jig for scribing and cutting the ends of an infill log panel.

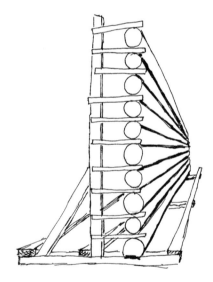

ASSEMBLING THE WALLS

When all these pieces have been prepared, the building can be assembled. Brace one corner post solidly into place and then move the first panel into position. Log panels can be scribed and fitted one piece at a time and the ends trimmed for the next post, but this can be slow. The panels are better constructed by building on a jig, then trimming and finishing the ends before the logs are taken down to cut the grooves. The jig will be a strong pair of uprights about two-and-a-half meters high that has two level sills under it. The first log, whether flattened or left round, is placed on the sills a short distance from the uprights. A centerline is snapped onto the log and plumb lines placed on the ends. A small spacer is laid on top and nailed to the upright and to the log. The next log is selected and placed in a like manner.

with care. The mortises in the sill and plate logs can be cut a little long so that the post can be wedged up tightly after each panel is in place. The groove (or dado) in the posts used to be cut with a narrow adze or framing chisel. Most often a chainsaw is now used for this operation, but I think a much better job can be done with

As you near the planned wall height, determine what your scriber setting will be. The total height of the assembly should be your predetermined height plus the accumulated scriber settings (which should all be the same for each log). Choose your last logs of a size to end up just right. Scribe all the logs and number them with tags, in sequence from the bottom.

Before they are brought down, the ends can be cut to length and the keyway or spline recess cut in. The ends are most often trimmed with a guide-equipped chainsaw, such as a Lumber-Maker or another of the various chainsaw guides available on the market. Place the guide-piece according to specifications. The only trick is to be sure that the cut is at right angles to the wall line. The dado can be cut with the chainsaw or a router. Bring the logs down and cut the lengthwise groove. The wall need not be reassembled until it is placed on the building. The post will have been blocked up to accommodate the settling height and will be hung into the top plate when that part is installed.

Use a seal such as EM SEAL at the ends. If the building is to be traditional in style, care must be taken that the mortises at the bottom do not fill with water. If there is a real danger of this, it may be prudent to drill a drain hole and seal a stub in the sill, then slide the post over this.

Windows and doors can be placed entirely within the panel, the same as in any other log building. If they are to be placed between the posts, it will be necessary to make provisions for settling allowance. Because the height of logs under the window is not great, there will be only a little settling and the top panel log can be slotted into the bottom window header. The top log can be treated in the ordinary way,

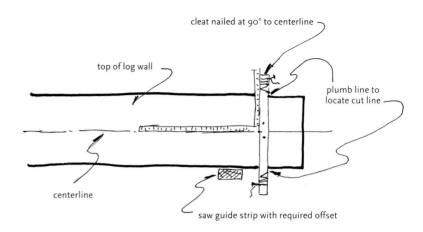

Use the centerline on the top of the wall to locate cut lines for the panel.

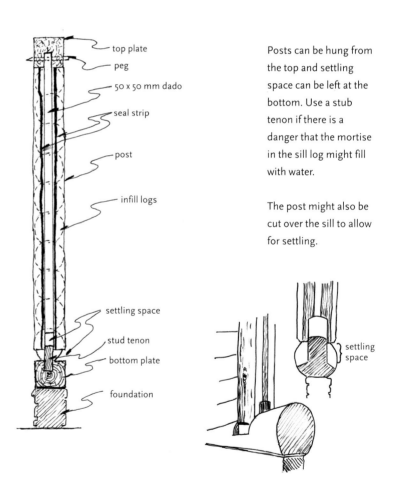

Posts can be hung from the top and settling space can be left at the bottom. Use a stub tenon if there is a danger that the mortise in the sill log might fill with water.

The post might also be cut over the sill to allow for settling.

Round-log post

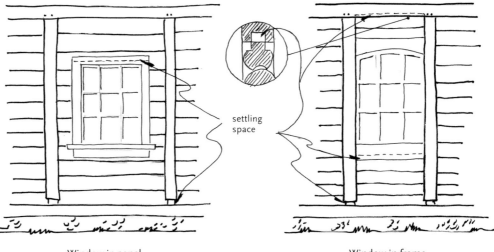

Two ways to place window openings in a log panel.

settling space

Window in panel

Window in frame

except that there will be less settling allowance needed.

Place the next post, complete with seal, and wedge it tight against the infill log-ends. Winch the top into place, then place the next panel. This can be continued until the wall is finished and the top plate has been placed. The other walls may be done in a like manner.

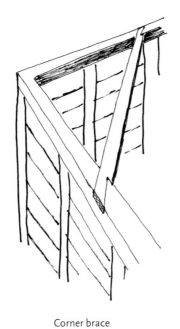

Dovetail a diagonal brace across the corner to prevent wracking.

Corner brace

Unless provision has been made to forestall it, this building will tend to wrack: the whole upper portion of the building twists in relation to the foundation. To avoid this, diagonal timbers can be dovetailed into the plate logs across the corners.

The use of log infill for post-in-the-sill-style buildings brought with it the problem of separation of the logs as they shrank and settled. When stone rubble was used as the infill, this was not the case. Because many of the original log buildings were large structures used for storage, the upper floor, where the settling took place, was not heated, and the only concern about the separation of the logs was the intrusion of weather and small animals. Several solutions for this problem have been tried, with different degrees of success. The solution outlined above is probably the most successful way to handle this tendency and is also the best way to apply this style to round logs.

PIECE-ON-PIECE VARIATIONS

Round logs may be used throughout the build-ing with just the posts flattened on each side. Because this style deviates from the traditional, I make the bottom join a little differently. In this case the post is on the outside and there is no place for water to accumulate. The use of saddle-notched corners also lends itself very well to this style of building and can produce a very large and strong building.

Another variation of this style is to use double posts and saddle-notched corners. This is a versatile system for building with logs of varying sizes: from very small to very large. If the top plate is constructed as shown in the illustration the entire building can be made from short logs that can be handled by one or two people. The only long pieces needed will be the tie beams at the top. This structure will also need diagonal bracing at the corners.

Piece-on-piece techniques are often used in conjunction with other styles of log build-ing in the basement area, additions and inte-rior divisions. Piece-on-piece bears a close resemblance to timber framing or post-and-beam construction. The greatest difference is in the style rather than anything basic. The intricate joinery of timber framing is still pos-sible with piece-on-piece and the log infill can have anything substituted from rock to stress skin panels.

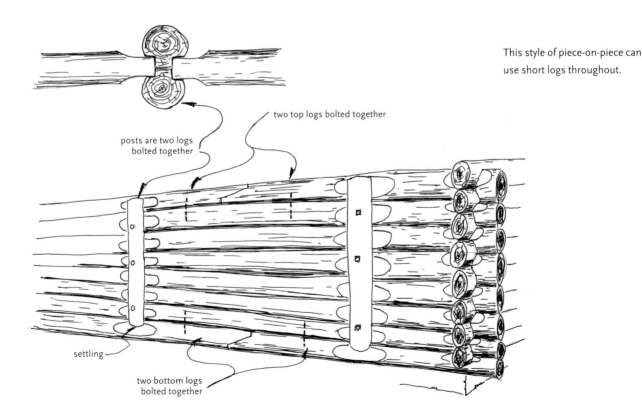

This style of piece-on-piece can use short logs throughout.

two top logs bolted together

posts are two logs bolted together

settling

two bottom logs bolted together

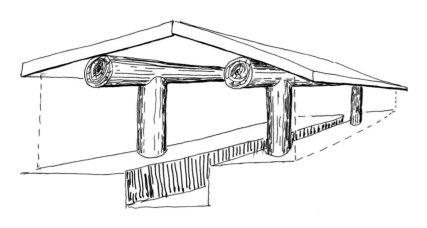

Longhouse configuration (west coast North America).

Post-and-Beam

Post-and-beam construction, like timber-frame construction, presents itself in a great many styles and varies markedly in appearance from one area to another. Consider post-and-beam as round-log construction for the purposes of this book. A very simple, and to me, a very appealing form of post-and-beam was constructed by the coastal people of the Pacific Northwest. This consisted of four gigantic posts with two equally gigantic beams on top that ran the length of the building. While this building embodies many features within its simplicity, the one I like best is that the beams are at the balance point of each half of the roof

Post scribed into the beam in post-and-beam construction.

Scribed mortise and tenon.

Log-end recessed into beam.

rather than acting as plates. This gives a natural balance to the whole structure.

Post-and-beam construction can be very simple or extremely complex, but the joints used are similar and useful in all forms of construction. If the surfaces to be joined are first flattened off, the joints, whether post, brace, bent or splice, are easier to lay out and cut. With good design, this kind of joint is perfectly acceptable and strong.

If the surfaces to be joined are to exhibit a round-log appearance, then the joints most often will have to be scribed. For best results, choose a post that is slightly smaller than the beam, or a girt that is slightly smaller than the post. A girt is a short beam that joins two bents, (frames that go across the building). A mortise and tenon can be started and the log-end scribed to match the beam or post. I am not fond of this joint because it has little compressive strength (see Posts and Purlins, Chapter 12).

The same appearance can be achieved by scribing the post into the beam as a housed joint. This can provide excellent strength and a good appearance suitable for many applications. A simplified version of this is to first flatten the receiver, then miter the post into this flat. The appearance is not quite as natural in some locations, but in others, such as a post to the ridge log, it can be totally usable.

Another join used for this purpose I call a post notch. It is very strong and has the best compressive capability. Braces are more difficult because it is harder to scribe at assorted angles than in a vertical position. One solution is to reposition the material until the scribe is vertical. Or you can use trial and error: take the scribe out in several steps, by cutting a little then retrying the fit.

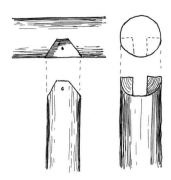

A style of post notch that is effective with large timber.

Another class of join is a splice. These will, of course, be avoided if possible. When it is not possible to avoid the use of a splice, there are a number of joints that can be used: scarfed, lapped, locked, wedged and shouldered. Whichever you choose, it will most likely be very noticeable, so choose a location and application that will appear structurally sound. For instance, a shouldered join in the middle of a floor joist would appear weak, while the same join over a post could appear very secure.

Another consideration is how to treat the panels between the uprights of a building framed with round logs. If the wood is very dry and stable, the opening can be framed and plastered. If the wood is not dry, the plaster may crack or separate. The posts can be flattened to take the framing, or they can be dadoed and splined, which I prefer. I am very much in favor of well-designed log-framed buildings. They have an excellent appearance, they are structurally superb and they can be built in a manner that conserves material and is environmentally kind. They may well, I hope, become a popular style of the future.

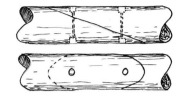

Simple lapped and bolted splice.

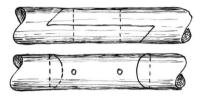

Lock and lapped splice.

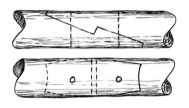

Shouldered splice. This works well for flatted joints.

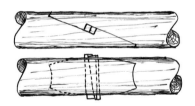

Lapped splice with wedges to tighten.

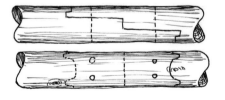

Shoulder splice.

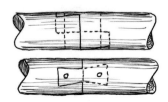

Dovetail splice.

CHAPTER 12

A ROOF OVER YOUR HEAD

Many years ago, when we first started the school of log building, I got a frantic phone call from a restaurant owner some distance away. He had hired a former student to build a new log restaurant, and when the walls had been skilfully completed, he asked his builder to put the roof on. The builder said he did not know how because he had left before that part of the instruction was reached. His question was, "Can you recommend someone who has completed the course?"

Needless to say, that problem comes up very rarely now because most students realize that the roof is possibly the most important part of the building and the sooner you can get the roof on your building, the less damage it will sustain from the elements. Once the roof is in place, the builder can relax a little and perhaps take a little time off. It would be very strange if any harm came to the building now.

As a matter of fact, a log building can benefit greatly by being left, at this stage, to settle and dry before finishing is undertaken. Many people cannot afford this luxury and will want to bring the house to lock-up as soon as possible. That is another problem; the main thing is that the roof is on.

This unusual diagonal truss across the center of a building illustrates the delight to be found in structural design.

There are two different types of roofs that might be used on a log building. A double-framed roof structure uses purlins and common rafters while a single-framed roof uses rafters or trussed rafters. A double-framed roof can have log gable-ends and purlins with log rafters or dimensional lumber rafters.

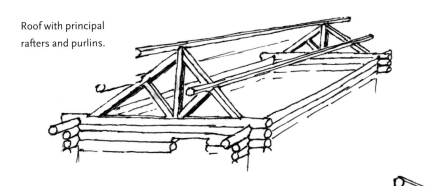

Roof with principal rafters and purlins.

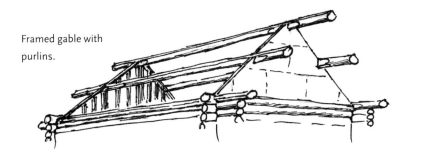

Roof supported by posts and purlins.

There are several different styles of roof within these types that are suitable for a log building. These might be trusses and purlins, posts and purlins, framed gables and purlins or a raftered roof without purlins. Or it may have trusses and purlins or post and purlin with the same rafters.

Framed gable with purlins.

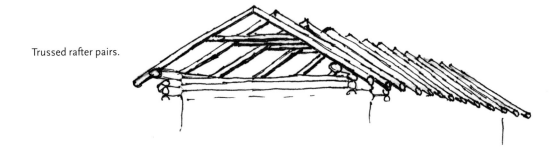

Trussed rafter pairs.

Log Gable-Ends

Let's start with the log gable-ends. Log gable-ends, like dovetail corners, are not approved by some building authorities. They may be right, but I wonder if it has ever been put to the test. Log gables, like round-notch corners, are the most natural way to build and, to my taste, more in harmony with the natural materials.

If the gable end is very high, it can look a little top heavy. For a low-pitched roof, log gables look snug and secure. Low-pitched log gable-ends present no settling problem, but a tall stack of logs can settle a significant amount. For this reason, when the roof line is high, most builders prefer the framed roof structure.

My preference is for a house that is deep in the woods with low-pitched log gable-ends, enormous purlins and ridge logs supporting a long overhang, and moss, great mounds of moss on everything. This is the kind of house I am building at Shanty Lake. (See Shanty Lake section.)

Building a log gable roof on the ground near the building can be an advantage. Take the cap log or the top log off the gable-end wall after it has been fitted. But first drive four nails, one in each inside corner of this log so that they are each the same height from the floor and also the height of the plate line on the side. Because you are going to use log rafters, the top of the plate log should be 100 to 150 mm higher than the plate line. This allows the rafter to be bedded down flush with the top of the plate log.

Measure the distance between the logs and the diagonal distance between the nails. This will provide the information you will need to block the pieces accurately in a position

Post-and-purlin roof support with extra pieces capping the posts.

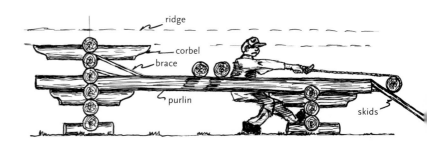

Move the top wall log onto the ground to prebuild the log gables.

relative to that which they occupied on the building. Also, place a good plumb line on the ends of each log to check the vertical position. A chalkline on the logs between the nails will provide the height of the plate line and you can take your measurements from there. If the roof has two purlins and a ridge, you can predict the height and location of each of these. Choose the purlins and ridge logs and put them to one side so that you can take measurements from them.

I like to build corbels (short supporting logs) under the purlins and ridge. These reduce the effective span of the purlins and increase the stability of the structure considerably.

Divide the span of the building into four equal parts between the centers of the plate logs. If the building is 7.2 m wide, each mark will be 1.8 m apart. If the slope of the roof is low, e.g., 6:12, then the rise of the roof will be 1.8 m and the top of the purlin will be at .9 m above the plate line. You will now have to

choose corbels and logs that will bring the purlins and ridge to these specifications.

Place the first corbels on the one-quarter mark and double scribe them for a square notch. They should be aligned accurately with the corresponding piece on the opposite wall and notched down about half their diameter. Scarf the top of the corbel and place the next gable log the same as a wall log with a lock notch. Now position a purlin between the gable ends. The challenge is to have the top of the purlin at the correct height and the top of the last corbel touching it at the bottom. This requires careful log-size selection.

Repeat this process with the ridge. Log rafters are not commonly used in log house construction anymore, but they are very strong and I admire their appearance. I lament the tendency toward plastic houses made of manufactured materials and I would rather my log house would not be confused with one of these. I want to build a house that is

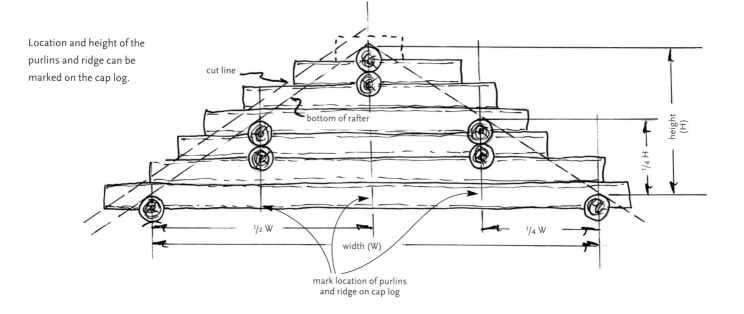

Location and height of the purlins and ridge can be marked on the cap log.

truly built of the woods and in so doing, I want to avoid the use of manufactured and synthetic materials as much as possible. Lumber is acceptable, but its use should be restricted to essential locations such as the floor. Particularly, I do not like to use plywood on a log house; it diminishes both the house and the trees.

Before you attempt to fit log rafters onto the roof, it is best that they be hewn to a uniform thickness. Choose the material to be as straight and as uniform as possible. Place all the rafters over two sills and cut them to the same length. Snap a chalkline across the ends to mark them all the same thickness (although the measurement at the butt end need not be the same as the measurement at the top end).

Turn this chalkline vertical, each rafter in turn, snap a line from end to end and hew each piece flat. Space the rafters on the plate log at 600- to 1000-mm intervals and double scribe them down to a line slightly below the top of the plate log. Scarf off the slope between the rafters.

Cut the top ends of the rafters so that they do not touch. They should be separated by a space equal to the settling you anticipate on the gable end. A roof with a gable-end height of 1.8 m can be expected to settle 1800:16, or 112 mm. Cut the top end of the rafter back about 60 mm on each side of the centerline.

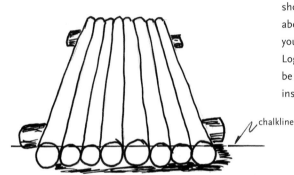

The top of the plate log should be about 150 mm above the plate line when you are using log rafters. Log rafters should be sized to make installation easier.

chalkline

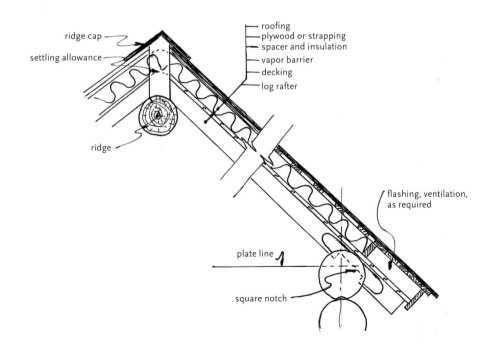

ridge cap
settling allowance
ridge

roofing
plywood or strapping
spacer and insulation
vapor barrier
decking
log rafter

flashing, ventilation, as required

plate line
square notch

Common types of log-
truss assembly.

Simple truss.

King-post truss.

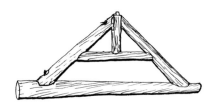

Collar-tie truss.

Queen-post truss.

W truss.

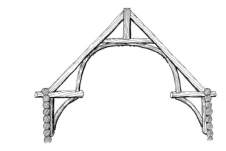

Hammer-beam truss.

TRUSSES

Now, let's consider trusses and purlins, post and purlins, framed gables and purlins or a raftered roof without purlins.

Trusses and purlins are, beyond question, the most popular style of roof structure, with posts and purlins a close second. Trusses do entail extra work and as such may be considered more expensive. If you are able to do the work yourself and have a good understanding of how to go about it, I do not think that the difference in time and money should cause you any worry.

Depending on what material is available, you may be able to build this roof system just as quickly out of logs on the site and save the cost of manufactured components. Framed gable ends with purlins is a style of roof system that is often favored by contractors and production yards. They can produce this type of roof structure more cheaply and it is quicker to move than trusses, which need to be reassembled.

For the buyer who may not have investigated different systems, this may seem like a logical proposition, but for a discriminating builder, this would not be the usual choice. For this reason, many of the commercial builders will quote the roof both ways, provide accurate information and let the buyer decide. With that in mind, let us first discuss the building of a king-post truss.

Trusses are classified according to their design. It may be a simple truss: a triangle with three cords. It may be a king-post truss, with a central post that will hold two purlin braces up. It may be a collar-tie truss that has a horizontal member about halfway up to support the weight of the purlins and also a short king-post to hold it up. A queen-post truss will be the same as the last with two additional uprights under the collar-tie. Or, as an alternative, you might choose to build a "W" truss, which has two king-posts and two purlin supports, or a hammer-beam truss, which is much like a collar-tie truss with additional purlin supports. Beyond this, you will be using bridge-type trusses and mechanical components. The other styles named can be made with wood pegs only or, as is more often the case, with minimal bolt connectors.

The king-post truss in the illustration is a very useful style and can be made quite quickly. You will need five logs and the top log off the gable-end wall. Prepare the five pieces, which will become the two principal rafters, the king-post and the two purlin braces.

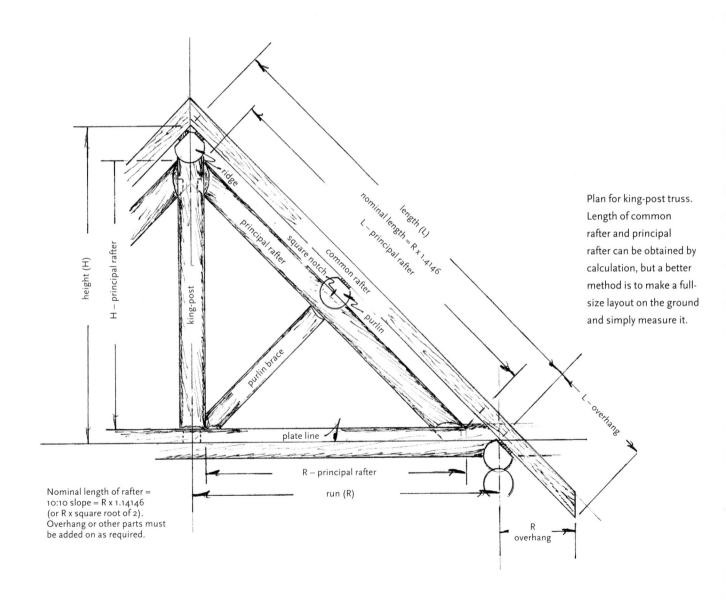

Plan for king-post truss. Length of common rafter and principal rafter can be obtained by calculation, but a better method is to make a full-size layout on the ground and simply measure it.

Nominal length of rafter = 10:10 slope = R x 1.14146 (or R x square root of 2). Overhang or other parts must be added on as required.

FIGURE 1

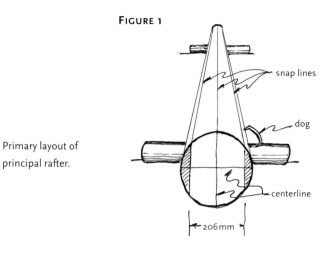

Primary layout of principal rafter.

snap lines

dog

centerline

←206mm→

FIGURE 2

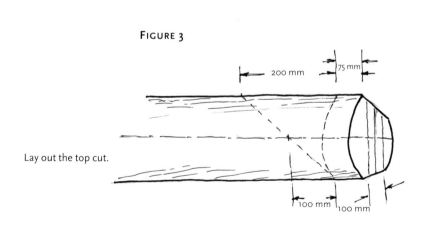

Square lines across the end.

FIGURE 3

Lay out the top cut.

200 mm

75 mm

100 mm   100 mm

Cut just slightly over length (200 mm) and flatten the straightest sides to a thickness of 200 mm. To do this, place the log across two blocks so that any bow is downward. Dog it firmly in place and snap a centerline down the middle in the usual way. Drop a plumb line down at each end (Fig. 1) and from this measure 103 mm each way and draw two more lines parallel to the centerline. In addition, draw a level line across the center of the log at right angles to the original centerline. I have added 6 mm to the overall thickness to make sure we have a full-sized component. Snap two more lines on the log, then roll it over and place the lines on the other side. Because you will be working from the centerline, it will not matter if the material is a little out of line or a little thick.

Hew or saw the log flat on the two sides. The reason this is cut flat is to provide a surface for eventual framing. Make sure that you do not encroach too much on the line: then you can choose to finish it with a hand or electric plane or leave the hewn surface. Place one of the principal rafters on blocks at a convenient height and from the end marks, place center-lines on the flat surfaces.

On the top end of the flat side that is to be the outside of the truss, place a mark 75 mm from the end (Fig. 2) with two squares. Carry this mark around the log to each of the center-lines. On the underside, drop back 200 mm and square a line across the work (Fig. 3).

You will find some templates very handy. Make these templates out of plywood that is about 9 mm thick. Cut the pattern with a high degree of accuracy and make one template for each size of tenon (Fig. 4). A large T-bevel, about 1000 mm long, will be useful to check angles (Fig. 5).

Lay out the width of the tenon on the end of the log (Fig. 3) and mark the cut lines with the square. Because our truss is a 1:1 slope (45 degrees), you can place a reference mark at 100 mm from the end line. In order that the angled line that you are marking will be on the right plane, make sure that the tang (short end) of the square is horizontal.

You now have your cut lines drawn (Fig. 3) and you can cut the angle on the end of the log. If you are at all unsure, cut 10 to 15 mm outside the line and finish with your slick. If a small mistake has been made, remember that you left a little extra length and you can remark the log a few millimeters and adjust the angle. Be careful, however, not to overcut into the tenon because it will be weakened. Remember, when you make the cut at the other end of the principal, you will not have this escape opportunity and your work will have to be correct.

Lay out and cut the tenon on the end (Fig. 6). This design is intended to be bolted together. Try your template over the tenon to check the thickness and then check the fit and accuracy of the angle by checking the angle of the template against the centerline. Measure the length of the rafter, with precision, to the bottom end and do a layout similar to the top end. When this has been cut, lay out and cut the seat for the purlin. The dimensions given are tentative and for purlin material that ranges from 250 mm to 300 mm in diameter. If your material is different, the width of the seat may have to be changed, but the depth of the cut should remain about the same.

Check all the sizes with the template and then bevel the corners of the tenons to prevent chipping. Measure the location of the

Making the bottom cut on a principal rafter for a king-post truss.

FIGURE 4

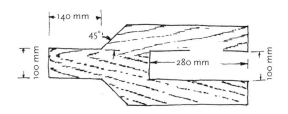

Use a template to check the dimensions.

FIGURE 5

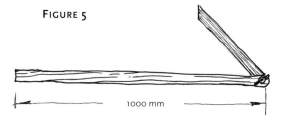

Large wood T-bevel. Used to check angles.

FIGURE 6

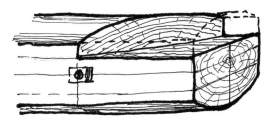

First cut on the top of the principal.

FIGURE 7

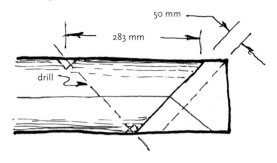

Shape the end of the principal.

FIGURE 8

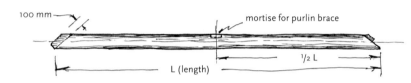

The completed principal rafter.

FIGURE 9

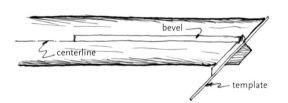

Checking the top angle with the T-bevel.

purlin brace (Fig. 8). Cut this mortise with a chisel because it is very small. Mark the center locations for the bolt drill-holes (Fig. 7). Drill from the inside toward the outside. It is best to chisel a flat spot from which to start the drill. If alignment is a problem, employ an offside observer to assist. When all the parts for the truss have been made and carefully checked with the template (Fig. 9), assembly should be a simple matter.

Because these parts are heavy and, in some cases, the assembly may take place up on the roof, I strongly recommend that all dimensions be checked most thoroughly. If the truss is to be put together on the building, a trial assembly might be first undertaken on the ground. Before the trusses are bolted together, there is an easy way to fit the purlins before anything is moved up onto the building. Position the principal rafters onto stump blocks about 300 mm high so that they are square and level. The centerlines should be exactly the same distance apart as the centerlines on the end cap logs, and the diagonals equal. One side at a time can be set up as long as the relative positions of the rafters are maintained.

Method of scribing the purlin to the principal.

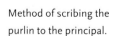

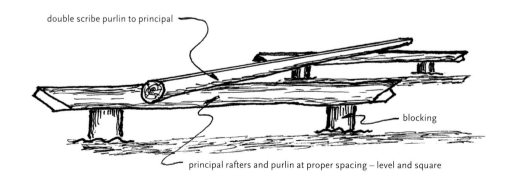

Purlins

Purlins are the parts of a double-framed roof that are intended to carry short lengths of common rafters that would span only the distance between each purlin, or from a purlin to the ridge. In this configuration then, the principal rafter will carry almost all the weight of the roof. The purlins will carry large sections of the roof load and the rafters only a small part of the total weight. This system is therefore much less efficient than a system composed of trussed rafters or common rafter pairs.

However, I am not concerned solely with efficiency, and the double-framed roof contributes greatly to the visual effect. After all, you want your building to be a place of delight as well as a place of firmness and commodity. For a moment then, think about the purlins.

The size of the purlin will depend on the distance it has to span, the pitch or slope of the roof and the load it has to carry. The load will be the dead load: the weight of the material used in the roof construction, including the weight of the purlin, plus the live load, which will be snow, wind or any other temporary load (this will vary from region to region). For this information consult engineering guides or log-span tables published by a log-builders association.

Having selected the purlins because they are large enough and straight enough, flatten them to a width of at least 150 mm in the usual manner. Next, place the purlin across the seats that are notched into the principal rafter. If there is a slight bow in the log, place it toward the top of the roof. Purists have stated that the bow of the purlin should be straight up, and I would agree with this if the log is to be left round.

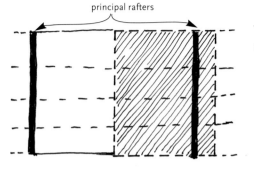

Load allocation for the parts of a double-framed roof.

Two principal rafters support 1/2 roof load.

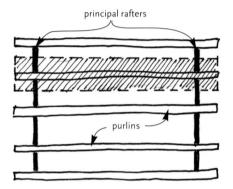

Purlin supports 1/4 of roof load.

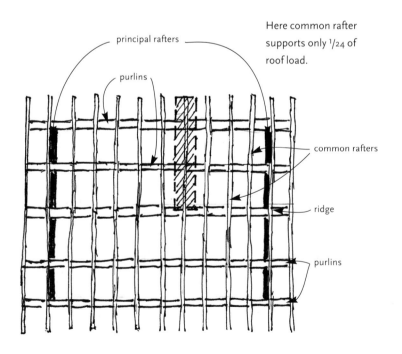

Here common rafter supports only 1/24 of roof load.

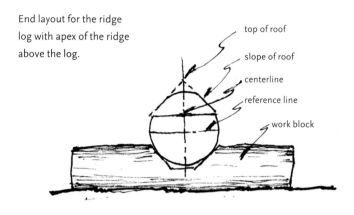

End layout for the ridge log with apex of the ridge above the log.

top of roof

slope of roof

centerline

reference line

work block

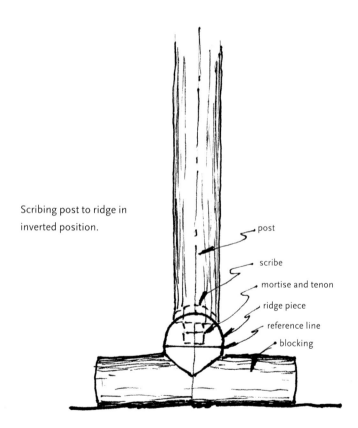

Scribing post to ridge in inverted position.

post

scribe

mortise and tenon

ridge piece

reference line

blocking

But, if you place the bow up and then flatten the log, you will weaken it in the center, where it can least tolerate weakening. The reason for the flat surface will become apparent later. In a style of roof that employs round log purlins, you can place the bow up.

Dog the purlin with the flat level and the centerline in the correct location. Take your scriber setting from a point 90 mm below the flat part of the purlin to the top of the rafter and double scribe the seat for the purlin as previously outlined. Leave as much material as possible in each notch. Greater strength could be maintained if you were to leave the purlin entirely on top of the principal, but this makes it difficult to secure and finish. As it is, you are leaving it 90 mm above the principal, which is a standard material dimension. If the setting for one end is more or less than the other end, the low end should be blocked up.

The ridge log is flattened on two faces, but if it is a little small on the top, *the flats need not meet*. Cut a flat seat 200 mm wide for the king-post that will leave the ridge at the specified height, in this instance, 227 mm. Make sure that there is sufficient overhang at each end. Cut a mortise for the tenon on the top of the king-post, 50 x 100 mm, and scribe the king-post down until the flats meet.

RAISING THE ROOF

With all the required trusses made and this additional work done, your roof system is ready to be assembled onto the building. If you have to rent a truck crane for the job, the truss can be put together on the ground and lifted into place, then the purlins and ridge lifted on and bolted. If you are working by hand, put enough planks or decking onto the upper floor so that you can work safely. Lift the truss pieces one at a time and assemble them on this floor. Roll the cap log and bolt it to the bottom of the truss.

Now, with the use of helper poles and guy lines, you can pivot the whole assembly into place. Brace the trusses solidly in place, because if the truss falls at this point, it could be a disaster. The purlins can be rolled or dragged up the rafter with two come-alongs and then bolted into place. The ridge can be treated the same way, except it will be necessary to temporarily extend the principal on the offside far enough to provide a lift point. Your roof system is in place.

POSTS AND PURLINS

A simple roof may consist of only two trusses, two purlins and a ridge. Or it may be bigger and have several trusses and more and longer purlins, in which case, a suitable splice may be used on the top of the truss. Other kinds and styles of trusses are made in the same manner, with the span and load governing the size of the logs. You may decide to use posts and purlins to replace one or all of the truss assemblies.

Raising a truss in place on the roof. Note the signal man standing in the "bight" of the line. Never stand in the bight!

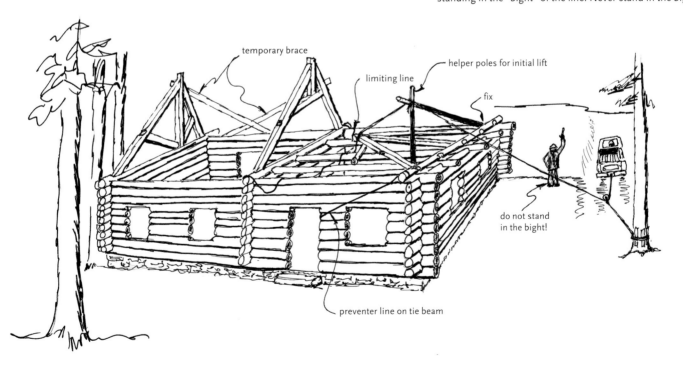

temporary brace

limiting line

helper poles for initial lift

fix

do not stand in the bight!

preventer line on tie beam

Various joins for post-and-beam:

More difficult
but strong and good
appearance.

Like the trusses, the posts are first cut and fitted to the purlins or ridge, then put into place. Use one or another of the post notches shown. The length of each post can be calculated from the plate line to the top of the ridge or purlin and precut to a finished condition. To erect this by hand, first stand up the posts in their right place and brace them. Secure large planks to the sides of the posts to form a ramp to the top. Place these planks low enough that the ridge or purlin can seat, then roll or drag the piece into place. If both sides of the building are not accessible, roll the far purlin to the other side of the house before putting up the posts.

The post may be fitted into the beam as a housed joint. This can provide excellent strength and a good appearance suitable for many applications. A simplified version of this is to first flatten the receiver, then scarf the post into this flat. The appearance is not quite as natural in some locations but in others, such as a post to the ridge log, it can be totally usable.

Strong, good appearance,
but needs scribe.

Strong and easy.

Easy and good appearance.

Strong and easy.

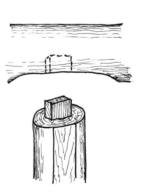

The material for the roof was on the site and indeed, right alongside the building. The first job was to put up the ridge log. This was to be a post-and-beam arrangement so I picked two posts and scribed them to the ridge while it was still on the work site. Paul came along to help with this because our equipment would now be extended to the limit. In fact I was not too sure that we would be able to get this big ridge log up into place, away beyond the reach of the old backhoe.

First, the posts. These were less than two meters long so they were not a problem. Mortises were already cut in the cap logs so it was only necessary to brace the post very securely in the right place. This done, we lifted the ridge log and put it across the building. The point of balance was marked and the distance from this point to the ends measured.

The hydraulics on the backhoe had sufficient power to lift the ridge, just not enough reach. We extended the reach by lashing a strong birch pole to the boom and then placed the machine in a position that brought the lift point over the centerline of the building, at a point equal distance from the end to the measured balance point on the ridge. All secure?

Once the metal roofing was in place on Knotingham, we finally had a dry place to sleep.

Jake and I have a coffee break.

Reach down, lift the ridge, turn it 90 degrees and lower it to the seats. It went just like that except it pinched Paul's hand a little as it snapped into place. I don't remember if we took the rest of the day off or not – we should have.

The next day we decked in the space between the wall and the outrigger on each side then started to put up the rafters. These are another couple of places where careful work will pay off. I am sitting upstairs wearing a T-shirt while I write this. It is 20° C below on the other side of the window.

The rafters are 2 x 6 spruce. I would rather have used log rafters but there are none close around here: we would have to go shopping for them and I wanted to get the roof on the house. The positions for the rafters were already marked on the plate and ridge so we just needed to lift them into place and skew nail them with big ardox nails (very long, twisted, ugly nails).

Next we put 2 x 4 strapping across the rafters to carry the metal roofing and the building was dry. Metal roofing is not pretty stuff, but it will allow the snow to slide off when the roof is steep enough and, above all, it is not a worry when sparks from the chimney land on it during one of those windy nights.

All and all, this took about a week. We were still living in our tents and

cooking on an open campfire. Time was pushing because I wanted to get the building livable and be able to lock it up before September, when I would have to leave for three months and come back to possible winter conditions.

Tony came by, and Charlene, another friend, and we put the floor down according to the plans. Tony stayed (he had little choice because he had come by canoe) and we did the gable ends, and with Fraser's help, insulated the roof and put in windows and doors.

We moved in, at least for the night. We were still cooking out under the tarp and fighting the raccoons for our groceries. Would you believe it? One night I got up to investigate an unusual noise and discovered a raccoon dragging away a full bottle of beer. He was going backwards and dragging it by the top. On reflection, I should have let him have it just to see how he planned to open it. At the time I was not prepared to make the sacrifice.

We built a Quonset hut from bent maple saplings to house our kitchen and storage. It lasted two winters.

CHAPTER 13

MORE ABOUT THE ROOF

TRUSS AND PURLIN SYSTEM

It is a matter of pride and also of practice and experience to be able to construct a roof-support system from drawings and specifications. If your interests and fulfillment lie in different areas, it is still possible to build a truss and purlin system very quickly using a more direct approach. This, out of necessity, is done mostly with a chainsaw. The best place to do this is right on the floor, or, if that is awkward, any flat and near-level area will do.

This is a collar-tie truss, and some layout will be required. First select a king-post or, if you wish, a king-post and a collar-tie. Cut the king-post about 500 mm longer than will be needed, set it on skids and snap a centerline. Draw the centerline on the log-ends and also a horizontal line in the middle. From these lines, draw two more each way: one pair each 50 mm from the centerline and the other pair each 100 mm from the centerline. Join the corresponding ends with chalklines, then cut the tenon on the large end of the king-post.

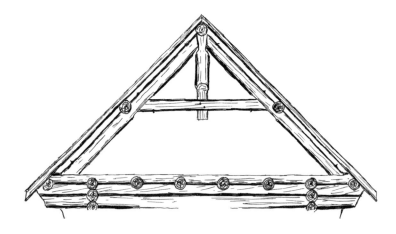

A quick and easy log truss.

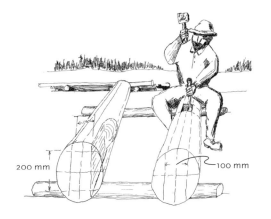

Lay out the collar-tie and king-post.

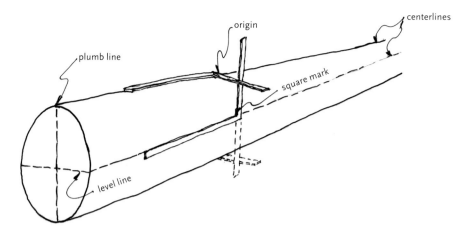

Use two squares to bring the layout accurately from one side of the log to the other.

The collar-tie is treated much the same way, but only one set of lines will be needed, the pair that are 50 mm from the centerline. Find the middle of the log and measure out the dimensions of the mortise each way from this center (e.g., 100 mm). Carry the center mark around the log either with a flexible strap or with two squares, and dimension the mortise on the other side.

Cut this mortise out. First score the cut lines with a chisel, then plunge-cut one halfway through from each side. Be careful to not over-cut the lines. Finish this off with a chisel or slick and test it for size with your templates.

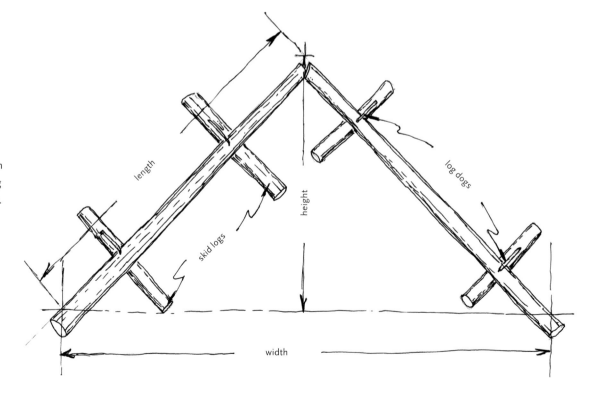

Place the principals on cross timbers and dog them firmly into place.

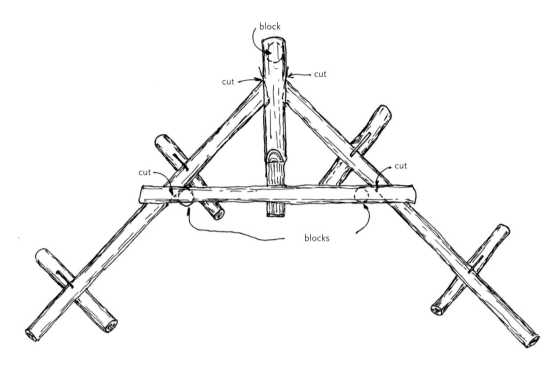

block

cut — cut

cut — cut

cut — cut

blocks

Place the king-post/ collar-tie assembly on top of the principals.

1) Position the assembled king-post and collar-tie on top of the principal rafters.
2) Block up as shown.
3) Make the four vertical chainsaw cuts through both parts in the locations shown with dotted lines.

Position the principal rafter pieces so that the top ends are roughly matched and the bottom ends are at the right width. This may best be accomplished by placing the pieces on timbers. If you are working on the floor, the plan of the truss can be laid out with chalklines. Dog these well into place or even nail straps across them to keep them from rolling. Put the tenon of the king-post just through the mortise on the collar-tie and place this assembly in position on top of the truss legs.

You are now going to cut these pieces together with the chainsaw. For this reason they should be blocked up with short stumps in such a way that they will stay in place after they have been cut. Cut straight down with the saw from the top of the king-post so that part of the cut is taken from each piece. These cuts should be angled in at the bottom about 5 degrees, so that the king-post can be driven

further to take up the space created by the width of the chainsaw cuts. Do the same at each end of the collar-tie. Locate the cut by eye or use a square to bring the cut locations up to the top.

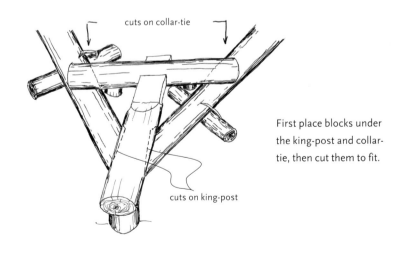

cuts on collar-tie

cuts on king-post

First place blocks under the king-post and collar-tie, then cut them to fit.

With this done, lower the king-post and collar-tie into the right place, then drill and bolt it to the principal rafters. You will need a long drill bit for this operation. You may drill through the principal from each side and mark the king-post, then lift this just enough to drill on through.

Measure the length of the principal from the centerline of the king-post on each side. Check the measurement to be sure that the rafters are indeed the right distance apart, then snap a chalkline across the bottom to locate the foot cut. If it is a king-post truss, be sure that the king-post is centered before you make this cut.

For the king-post truss, nail planks across near the bottom, then cut in the purlin braces. This may be done by cutting the slope on the bottom end then cutting the top end. A short tenon should be left at the top to hold the purlin brace in position. This truss is not quite as strong or as neat as the previous construction, but it can be quite adequate.

POSTS AND PURLINS

As another alternative, you might decide to use posts and purlins to replace one or all of the truss assemblies on the building. Like the trusses, the posts are first cut and fitted to the purlins or ridge, and then put into place. Use one of the post notches (See Chapter 12) and leave the bottom end of the post long until the notch has been fitted.

Finally, the length of each post can be calculated from the plate line to the top of the purlin or ridge and cut to a final length. To place this roof system on the building with a crane is very easy. It is also possible to put it in position by hand. To do this, first stand the posts up and brace them well. Then secure large planks to the sides of the posts to form a ramp to the top. Place these planks low enough that the ridge or purlin can be seated without moving the plank, and far enough beyond the ridge post that you have a purchase point from which to lift the ridge.

You can now roll or drag the ridge and purlins into place. If both sides of the building are not accessible, roll the purlin intended for the far side to the other side of the building before putting up the posts.

GABLE ENDS

I am not especially fond of framed gable ends on a log house. The less manufactured material used, the better. Your original undertaking was to build a house that put the least demand on the environment, and at this point perhaps you should renew your commitment to that ideal. However, framing can be accomplished with natural materials, so I will take a short look at how this is done in the industry before I talk about substitutes.

This gable end can be constructed in place or on the floor and then raised into place. It is a standard structure with multiple studs under the square cutouts allowed for the ridge and purlins. The ridge and purlins are, in turn, scarfed down square at these points. After the gable ends have been well braced into place, the logs are dropped into these recesses. Commercial builders use this style of roof because it is cheap in terms of the labor required to build it and move it, but it is questionable whether the personal home builder would obtain much advantage from using this type of gable. The post and purlin system that I discussed earlier is the obvious substitute. The spaces between the posts can be framed in place and sheathed in plywood, siding, shakes or one of many other materials.

Trussed Rafters

Trussed rafters are a very different class of roof system. These pairs of rafters can be brought to a high degree of finish and to complement almost any building design. Trussed rafters are simply rafter pairs, smaller than principal rafters, that are positioned on the building at intervals that do not require purlins. These intervals could be from one-half to two meters, depending on the roof-decking material. These rafters can be plain and rugged or highly finished. They can be simple or they can be decorative.

You might want to consider using trussed rafters because they are lighter and more easily handled by an individual working alone. These roof structures were originally designed for masonry buildings with substantial wall thickness, because they rely in part on the rafter seating on the outside of the wall and the support struts resting on the inner part of the wall. A log building with an outside plate can duplicate this and such rafter pairs can be worked to good effect. Traditionally, roofs of this nature and the one following would be constructed

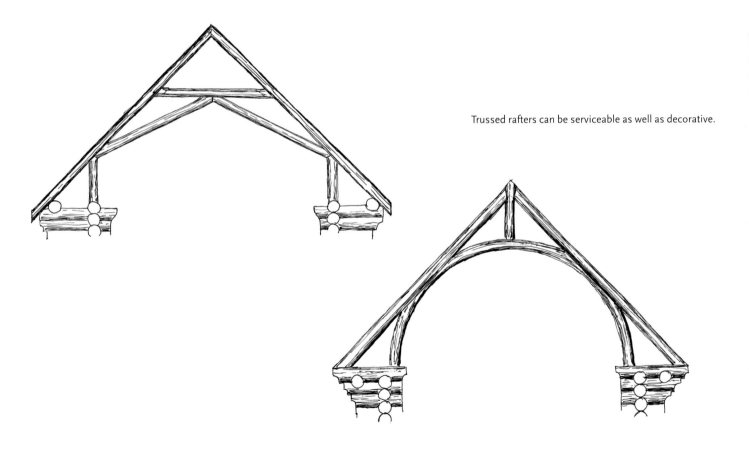

Trussed rafters can be serviceable as well as decorative.

Trussed rafter roof over south porch of Heckington Church, Lincolnshire, England.

from dressed material and decorated with moldings and carvings to the designer's and builder's satisfaction. Such a roof can be constructed from round materials that have been carefully selected for size, quality and form and fitted with the scribed or scarfed joins I have already talked about.

Hammer-Beam Roof

The next division of roof you might consider is a hammer-beam roof. This roof is very much like a trussed-rafter roof, used when the wall is not wide enough for trussed rafters. The support for the plate piece is given by a curved brace originating further down the wall. This roof can also be made of round material. The plate piece, or hammer, may be long and extend into the building. It derives much of its ability from the curved braces that start below the plate. This roof can also be built with a short hammer and the brace made in one piece from the rafter. This style of truss is always associated with a double-framed roof: a roof that has principal rafters, purlins and common rafters. There is no reason that these rafter pairs could not be alternated with simpler designs in order to avoid an otherwise overdone effect.

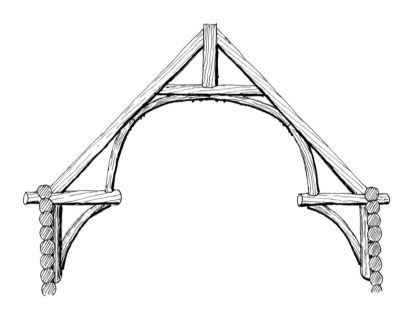

Hammer-beam truss in round wood.

The Finish Work

With the logwork done, you are starting into another phase of the building process, which in many ways is quite different and yet it is still closely related. This work connects directly to what you have already done, because the quality of your finish work and the ease with which it can be done depends on how well organized the original logwork was.

Before placing the common rafters and covering on the roof, see that all cutouts and preparation have been completed for the second floor. This work should be done while it is still easily accessible so that you will not have to try to do logwork in an awkward and confined position. If the roof is extended out beyond the wall to an outside plate, make sure that there is a seat cut all around to receive the floor decking. Check the electrical plan to be sure that any drilling or cutouts for wires are done. And cut seats for the filler between the plate, purlins and ridge.

Decide whether you want the ceiling material to run the length of the roof or the length of the rafters. In the former case, you can use a 18-mm spacer on top of the purlins and ridge. If you wish the finish boarding to go the same direction as the rafters, use a 35-mm spacer so that a nailing strap can be placed on the bottom of the common rafters. Let's assume that you are going to run the boarding across the rafters and with the length of the building. Place the 18-mm spacer strip down the gable ends and along the ridge and purlins. The plate will have a thicker spacer (40 mm) to key the rafter. The sawn rafters will be placed on top of this. These rafters will extend beyond the eave to form the overhang and they can be notched over the spacer strip at the plate.

An extra rafter can be placed at either side of the gable to provide backing for the ceiling and soffit. In areas of high winds, it will be necessary to use metal cleats or other approved connections to fasten the rafters. The size of the rafter will depend on the amount of insulation required. In areas that require R-40 insulation, it is almost necessary to use a 2 x 10 rafter. The width of the eave line can be reduced by taking a wedge off the bottom of the rafter. The shape of the roof can be altered by cutting and shaping the rafter.

Place eave blocking along the plate at the outside. This blocking should stop about 50 mm from the top of the rafter to allow for air circulation.

Roofing Materials

The simplest thing to do now is deck the roof over with whatever materials you have chosen and cover it with a light roofing paper awaiting the finished, insulated roof. The roof can be insulated with fiberglass or foam placed between appropriate spacers. The roof can then be strapped or sheathed and any roofing you want can be applied. For our house I would like to use cedar shakes. There are other kinds of roofing that also go well with a log house, and for reasons of supply, location or taste you may choose one of these others. Shakes are good in a northern climate and in the woods where there is shade, and they have the advantage that the builder can make them himself. The disadvantage is, that like all wood products,

Log gable-end showing the slot where roof decking will settle.

metal roof is that you will never have to shovel the snow off it.

I do not think rolled roofing or thin paper (asphalt) shingles have a good appearance for a log house, but they can be used as a temporary measure until a better material can be made or purchased. Perhaps that is also why they do not give a satisfactory appearance: because they appear temporary and the house itself does not, there is a conflict.

they are damaged more by constant sunlight than anything else.

Clay or concrete tiles make good roofing material in milder climates and perform well where there is a lot of rain and humidity. Tiles provide a good weight to hold their position if high winds are a possibility and they have a heavy shadow line that is in keeping with the weight of the building.

Sheet metal makes good roofing, but not the thin, flimsy stuff: use a good heavy gauge with distinct rib lines. One advantage of a steep

CEDAR SHAKES

Cedar is considered to be the most suitable species for the manufacture of shakes, although, in the past, many other kinds of wood were also used with good results. Among these were oak, walnut, spruce, pine and almost any species that had clear wood and a straight grain.

Shake bolts are rounds about 600 mm long that are cut off the end of the log and split into segments small enough to be handled. Place the bolt in an upright position and cut slabs off with a froe. Taper is obtained by turning the block over on each cut. There are machines that can do this job with power, but if you have good material, one person can produce a great many shakes in a day. All you need for tools is a froe and a heavy mallet. It is satisfying work.

The building code allows shakes to be used on a fairly shallow roof and requires that a perforated paper be placed under each course (row). I feel that both of these decisions are faulty. The shakes last much better on a steep roof and are less inclined to leak from backed-up water. Also the undercourse of paper contributes to decay for lack of ventilation. Under

8 kg nylon or teflon mallet

froe

suggested splitting pattern

drive froe only a short distance

600 mm

cedar shake bolt

Cedar shakes can be used if your climate is suitable. They do not last well in a hot or humid environment.

reasonable conditions, shakes will last a long time if they have adequate ventilation.

To use cedar shakes, first sheath the roof with 12-mm plywood, then apply the shakes. If the local building code will allow, use 2 x 4 strapping at 225-mm intervals up the roof to nail the shakes to. This allows better ventilation and the shakes will last longer. The eave will have to be closed in solid for a distance of 600 mm to avoid wind damage. You should put blocking between the strapping to prevent insect and rodent entry. After that an extra rafter is hung beyond the purlins and faced off with a barge board so that the ends of the purlins are covered.

To apply the shakes, start with a double course that extends about 50 to 60 mm beyond the roof. Lay the next row with about 250 mm to the weather. Shakes are approximately 610 mm long, and about 360 mm are covered by the next row, leaving 250 mm exposed. Nails are placed approximately 300 mm up the shake

and are thereby covered by the following course. In other words, don't place nails only 200 mm from the end of the shake. Make sure that the nail heads are covered and that the shakes are spaced about 6 mm apart, because they expand when they are wet. Avoid walking on them as much as possible. If they have a tendency to split when you place the galvanized nails, spray them with water for a while before you use them.

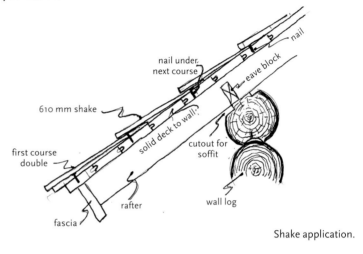

Shake application.

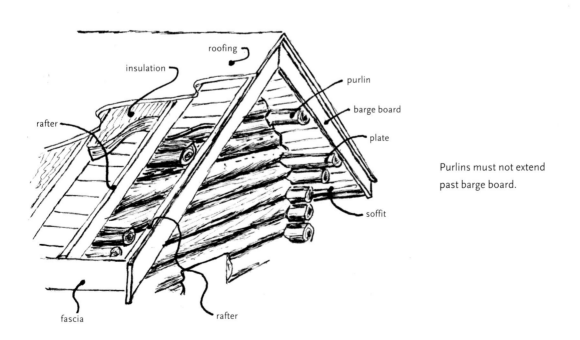

Purlins must not extend past barge board.

COMPLETING THE INSIDE

To complete this particular style of roof you will now move inside. Drill and install rough wiring, which may require distribution behind the ceiling. Install the insulation, which will be friction-fit fiberglass batts and a polyethylene vapor barrier. This should all take only a short time and not a great deal of money, but the comfort dividends will be considerable.

The next part will take a little longer and you will be glad that you placed the spacer strip on top of the logwork. This spacer has lifted the rafter high enough so that you can slide the ceiling tongue and groove material onto the top of the plate, purlin or ridge as you come to them. This will not only save time and effort, but it will make a better looking job.

If the logwork has gone well and quickly through the winter or summer and the roof has been finished, the logs will not be soaked with water and discolored. This will make the big job of cleaning the logs much easier and faster.

Post-and-purlin roof-support system with the cutouts for ceiling, outrigger insulation and upper-floor decking all in place.

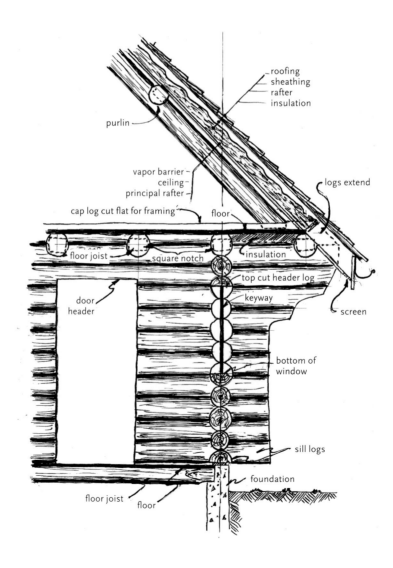

CHAPTER 14

WINDOWS, DOORS, LOG-ENDS AND STAIRS

When we first started the school of log building, the ordinary practise when installing doors and windows was to spike a dimensional header to the cut log-ends. This piece reached right up to the top of the opening in order to prevent the door from binding as time went on and the building settled. The only thing wrong with this is that as the building settles, the logs loosen and appear to be draped over the doors and windows. One of our main objectives was to teach students how to build openings that were stable and strong, yet allowed vertical movement. This concept was easily understood and over the years has been developed to a very acceptable level.

WINDOWS

The window sizes will have been specified on the building plan before you started and the units, or the materials to make them, will be on the site. The openings will be a little smaller than the size of the window or door. The header

log should have been cut to the right size as I discussed in Chapter 9.

If you are ordering custom-made windows and doors, it is well to do this a good period in advance, because most suppliers require at least six weeks to fill an order. You can order the sash with or without a frame and you should specify that they will not have a brick molding.

It is well worth a visit to your window dealer before the building has reached the height of the bottom of the windows. They often have units in stock that are surplus and available at a saving. You would then be able to tailor the openings to suit these windows. If you have the opportunity and a place to work, it is also possible to make your own window sash. You can buy surplus sealed units only and make the sash and frames to suit.

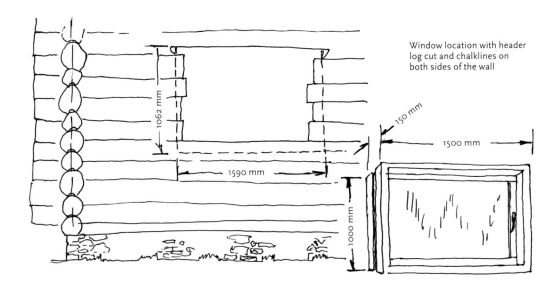

Window location with header log cut and chalklines on both sides of the wall

Layout for window opening to allow for headers and settling.

CUTTING THE WINDOWS

Let's say that the window frame you have measures 1000 mm high, 1500 mm long and 150 mm wide. The stock for the headers is 45 mm thick. This stock will be cut to 150 mm wide and 1000 mm long. You will need two pieces.

The header log for this location will be cut 1590 mm wide and the upper flat will be about 2100 mm from the floor. I say "about" 2100 mm because at times you will want to alter this height a little in order to secure a better position on the header log. Mark in the vertical cut lines for the window by means of a level or chalkline. Mark in the bottom cut, which will be 1062 mm lower: 1000 mm for the window and an additional one-sixteenth (62 mm) for settling space. If you have trouble projecting a straight vertical line onto the curved logs with the level, use a plumb bob with a thin line and project a shadow onto the wall with a strong light directly in line behind it to give the locations.

To make these cuts freehand with either a chainsaw or a handsaw is very difficult. I have had people declare that they can indeed do this, but it turns out that they are willing to accept a lower standard. If you are using a chainsaw, use a chainsaw guide on it and place the guide track plumb and parallel to the centerline of the wall. Have the saw sharp and cutting very straight, then try to make the cut all in one operation. To do this you will have to position yourself at just the right height so that the saw can be pivoted through at the top, where the header log has

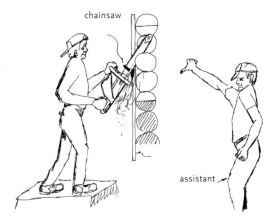

chainsaw

assistant

Use a saw guide to make clean square cuts on the side of the window or door.

been cut out, then continue slowly to the bottom of the cut. Check constantly that the saw is at right angles to the wall.

Another way to do this is to use a padded saw with two guide boards suitably placed. This operation generally requires two people, one to run the saw and the other to tend the off-end of the saw blade. By this means it is possible to obtain an extremely accurate cut.

If you are using a handsaw, you can place two upright guides, one on each side of the wall, and just graze these with the cut. A well sharpened handsaw will produce a much finer cut than a chainsaw and do it quite quickly too!

It should not be necessary to sand these log-ends but an electric angle grinder might be used to even out any irregularities that appear.

The bottom cut is easy. If you are using a chainsaw, first cut out a small section, about 20 mm wide at one end, then plunge-cut the saw through at this end so that you can see the progress of the blade as it goes through. Keep your cut about 15 mm above the line, then brush to the line after the cut is complete.

If you are using a handsaw, cut down to the line at intervals of about 150 mm and split off the blocks, then use your slick across the log to come as close to the line as you can. The resulting flat can then be planed or sanded to an acceptable finish.

If your sash has a frame and a sill, you may have to cut the bottom to a similar slope. If it does not have a slope, you should cut a step and slope outside the window frame.

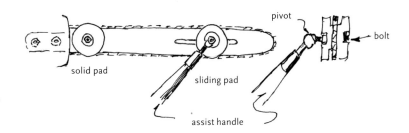

A true and accurate cut may be obtained with a chainsaw equipped with guide pads. These are now available commercially, or they can be made. Ed Miller, PO Box 868, Gatlinburg, IN, 37738, USA makes an excellent guide pad that I highly recommend.

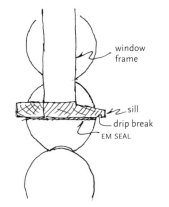

Windowsill should have a slope and a drip break.

THE KEYWAY AND SPLINE

A keyway and spline are used to keep the unsupported log-ends in place and at the same time allow them to settle. There are two ways to do this.

Make a single chainsaw cut down the log-ends near the centerline to accommodate an angle iron key. The cut will measure 50 x 50 x 4 mm thick. For doorways or larger windows, I like to use a wood spline and for this you will have to make multiple chainsaw cuts. If you are not using a chainsaw, you can drill the back of the keyway with a 50-mm auger and chisel the keyway out at each log-end as the building goes up.

Dado the spline into the header plank that you previously prepared, place a sealing strip (EM SEAL, sill seal, fiberglass, etc.) on the log-ends, and install the header pieces. The spline should slide easily into the keyway with just enough interference to prevent it falling out again. If you have to drive it in, it will have a tendency to start the log-ends splitting. If the wood you are using has a spiral grain or a tendency to check, you can countersink and bolt through each log-end just behind the spline to prevent this. This is not often done with cedar logs unless they are very short, but when using Douglas fir, pine or spruce, it could be useful.

Chainsaw cutting sequence for keyways.

Fig. 1 – Lay out cut lines on log-ends.
Fig. 2 – Cut to depth of key piece and 25 to 38 mm for insulation and electrical wires. The sequence shown is efficient for chainsaw work.

FIGURE 1 **FIGURE 2**

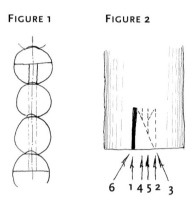

When using a standard header piece, the key piece itself may be a 2 x 4 or an angle iron. I generally prefer the metal key piece.

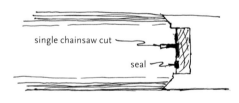

single chainsaw cut

seal

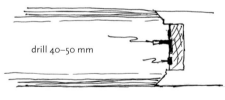

drill 40–50 mm

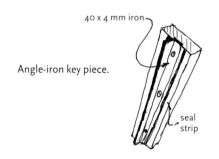

40 x 4 mm iron

Angle-iron key piece.

seal strip

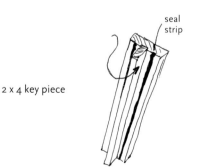

seal strip

2 x 4 key piece

Trim and Skirting Boards

Cut a short distance back into the log at the width of the header board to provide a seat for the trim board. If you are using your own or custom-made windows with heavy frames that do not require a header board, and if you have made an accurate cut, you may elect to omit the trim board altogether.

You will need a skirting board at the top to enclose the settling space. Leave this to the very last so that as much of the expected settling will have taken place before this piece is installed. I like to use a thicker board for this job with cutouts at each end to allow the trim board to slide up behind it as the building settles. If the skirting is in the right place, it will likely not need adjustment. Nevertheless, secure it with screws so that it can be removed for alteration if required.

Another way to do this is to install a skirting board that is laminated in such a way that the laminates can be removed one at a time as needed. Yet another method, if the logs are big enough, is to recess the trim board into the header log. This recess would be cut at the same time that the log is fitted.

It is a good idea to keep in mind that the trim boards at the top should exhibit some uniformity after the building has settled. While one smaller window might require only 30 mm of settling space, a larger window may require 150 mm. In most instances, you would use the width of board required for the larger window for all of the windows.

Still another approach to dealing with the settling of doors and windows is to use a substantial trim piece around the three sides of the frame. These trim pieces will be strong enough

Decorative window trim on a bay window.

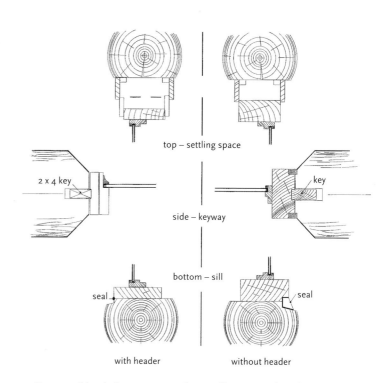

Two possible window treatments for installation. Good workmanship is still the best insurance.

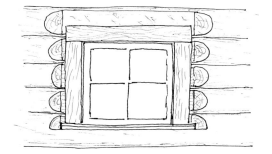

A heavy window trim can take the place of a key piece.

to hold the log-ends in place and the ends as well as the top log would have to be cut to match the width of the frame.

The part of the log-ends that protrude beyond the frame should be planed or sanded to a finished condition. The ends can be left square or they can be scarfed off at an appropriate angle. For my part, I like to leave them square and to keep the trim width to a minimum or, if possible, avoid the use of trim altogether.

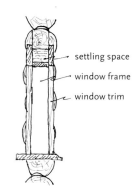

settling space
window frame
window trim

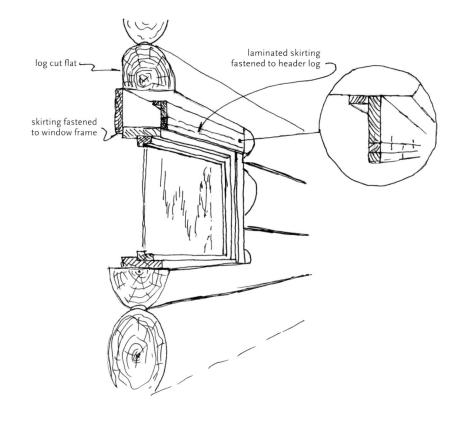

log cut flat

laminated skirting fastened to header log

skirting fastened to window frame

One proven method of installing settling boards. This might be the very last job to do on the building.

SOME UNOBTRUSIVE FRAMES

A style of window and door frame that I like to make is designed to be as unobtrusive as possible. I will describe a door here for a change, although windows can be done in the same way. This style has to be assembled in place.

The door frame and the header for the log-ends are the same piece. The size of the material will depend on the size of the logs or the style of the frame. I have found that a door frame that measures 200 mm by 75 mm is suitable. Thicker pieces tend to check too much and thinner ones are unsubstantial. The sides of the frame have a key piece that is dadoed into the back and fastened from the back. At the top there is a tenon that will position the head piece. The log-ends should be well cut to fit against this frame with the least possible irregularity.

Place the same seal on the log-ends as we did in the previous example, start the key into the slot at the bottom and then slide it up against the log-ends and into place. Jam a temporary spacer in between these frames at the bottom until you are finished, when the spacer can be replaced with the sill. Slide the head piece into the space left at the top for settling, then lower it onto the tenons on the top of the side pieces. Drive the pegs into place. Except for the top skirting, the frame is now complete and requires no trim. The door may have been pre-hung and can now be reinstalled.

Windows, either opening or fixed, can be made the same way and a skirting board

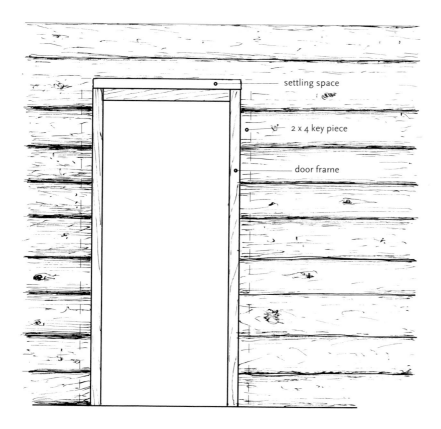

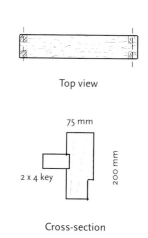

Top view

75 mm

2 x 4 key

200 mm

Cross-section

A heavy door or window frame can be used instead of log-end headers. This frame is assembled in place.

A style of heavy door framing that works well.

Door frame.

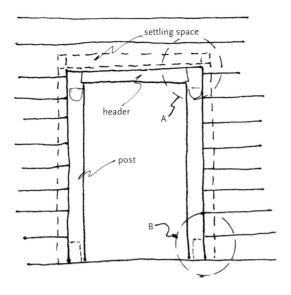

settling space

header

A

post

B

A: Top of post.

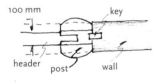

100 mm

key

header   post   wall

B: Bottom of post.

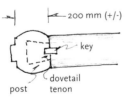

200 mm (+/-)

key

dovetail
tenon

post

Side view: top of post.

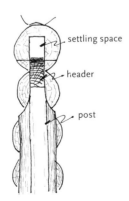

settling space

header

post

installed at the top. These frames are extremely solid and satisfactory.

Another frame that has a good appearance is made in much the same way. The frame is a pair of heavy slabs cut from the center portion of a log and the edge left natural. It will have the key piece dadoed into the back and a tenon on the top. The tenon is just entered into a mortise in the top or header log to permit settling. A jam strip is dadoed into the face of this frame as a door stop and the door can be hung in the usual way.

Still another way, and one I am very fond of, is to flatten two sides of a post and fit a top header-piece that will measure about 100 by 200 mm. The post has a scarf on the top end to bring it to the same width and a keyway dado in the back.

FINISHING

When the windows and doors have been installed, the house is to the lock-up stage. With a log house, this is very near to a finished house because, if you have been careful to keep the logs clean, there would seem to be very little "finishing" to do. As a matter of fact, people often do move in at this stage and complete the finishing as opportunity presents itself. Unfortunately, the disruption of the household by sanding and sawing tends to slow the work badly, and there is a tendency to overheat the new structure. I would recommend that the moving in be left until everything is complete.

Log-Ends

The overall appearance of a log building is, of course, affected by a number of factors. One of these factors will be the style, shape and treatment of the log-ends.

In the old days, log-ends might be cut very close to the corner so that they were less inclined to become wet with snow or rain. At times they were ignored altogether and left at random lengths, the way they came from the woods. This aspect of building with logs, like all others, has come into focus, and a variety of forms and treatments have been developed to deal with log-ends.

First, as each log is placed on the building, log-ends should be cut a little longer than the final planned length, say by 50 mm. The log-end should then be painted with linseed oil or an emulsified wax solution as each log is fitted. This will reduce the tendency to check at the log-end, which is caused by the rapid drying of the short portion between the end of the log and the notch.

Second, the log-end should be carefully coved all the way from the end to the notch. Too often someone forgets and cuts a deep V-groove right to the log-end or cuts a groove too near the end and then does a short cove. Either way, an unsightly groove will mar the appearance of the log-ends. The more nearly uniform the cove at the log-end appears, the better will be the overall appearance of the wall.

If the logs are cut short and straight down the wall, the building will tend toward a formal or even severe look. This might be right for some buildings but a bit strange for others. If the log-ends are cut very long, the effect is quite different. If the log-ends are sloped or

If log-ends are balanced well enough they will sometimes fall together, which can be dangerous.

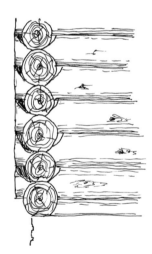

Two possible log-end treatments. The overall appearance of a log building is affected by the style, shape and treatment of the log-ends. Use your imagination.

Log-ends straight cut and short.

Rough-hewn log-ends.

Effect of slope on log ends:

Sloped in at the bottom lightens the feeling of the building.

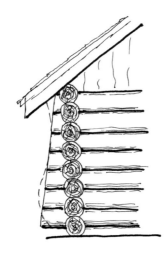

Sloped out at the bottom attaches the building to the ground.

Short, straight ends impart a formal or even severe appearance.

curved in toward the bottom, the effect is to lighten or lift the house, but if they are sloped in at the top, the effect is to attach the house more firmly to the ground.

Curves and sweeps can be entertaining, but sometimes they become too fussy and give me an uneasy feeling. The logs can be beveled, scarfed, hewn, pointed or random, just to mention a few of the alternatives. In some locations they are even painted in variegated colors.

Whichever style you choose will influence the tone and style of your building. The best way to decide is to go back to the system you used in your original planning: look at as many buildings as you can and then do what you want.

Sand the log-ends smooth. An angle grinder is the most suitable tool for this. However, if you have cut the log-ends with a handsaw, it is possible to do this job by hand. The important thing is that the rough-end grain be smoothed out so that it will be less inclined to absorb water. Use linseed oil or some other sealer on the ends to obtain your final finish.

STAIRS

Many log houses suffer from the lack of a well-built stairway. This is not all a bad thing. Many of these staircases, while certainly not standard, do show a lot of imagination. If they can also be well constructed and follow a few safety guidelines, they will become a credit to the builder.

When planning a house, leave enough space for the stairway and landings on the plan, and then you will not be disappointed when some other space has to be sacrificed to make the stairs possible. Also keep in mind that the house will settle and the stairway will have to accommodate that.

There are three types of stairs that are in general use. A straight stair, as the name implies, has a straight run from the upper to the lower landing. A platform stair has two or more runs at any angle to a platform or landing. A curved or spiral stair is often designed into a building, but not as frequently built.

Three styles of stair.

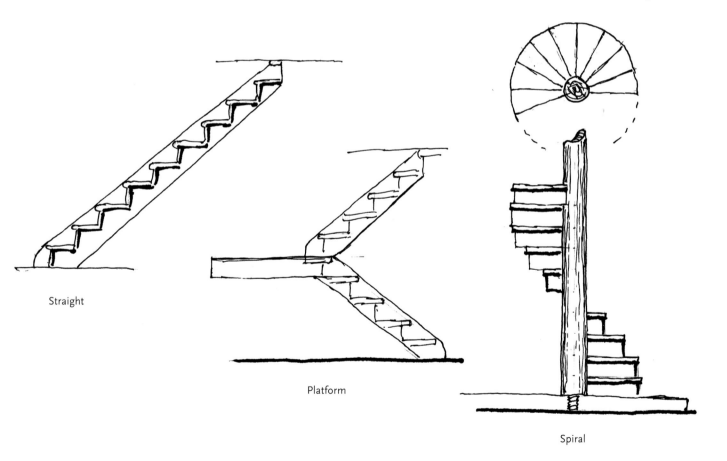

Straight

Platform

Spiral

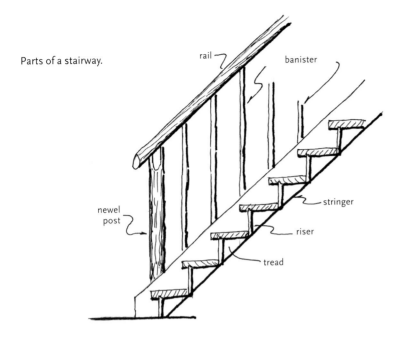

Parts of a stairway.

rail

banister

newel post

stringer

riser

tread

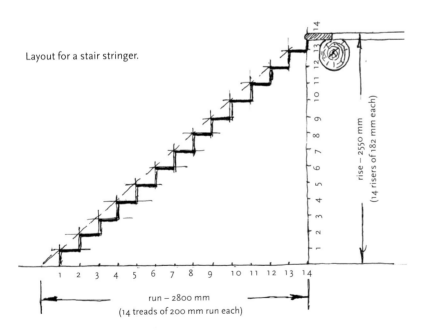

Layout for a stair stringer.

rise – 2550 mm
(14 risers of 182 mm each)

run – 2800 mm
(14 treads of 200 mm run each)

The parts of a stairway are as follows. The stringer is the part that supports the tread, and can be either housed or open (as with a stair horse). The tread is the part you walk on and the riser is the plank that fills the space between the treads. The rail is the hand-hold and the newel post supports the rail.

Stairs are specified as to the run, the rise and the number of risers and treads. The run is the horizontal space occupied on the floor; the rise is the height from one landing to the next; and the number of risers will indicate the number of treads.

For a stair to be safe, it should have a comfortable relation between the rise and run of each tread. As a rule of thumb, this relationship can be close to 400 mm for the combined run and rise for each tread, but the tread must be 200 mm minimum. The run could be, for example, 250 mm and the rise 150 mm.

The space between treads, if they are left open, should not be large enough for anyone to accidentally allow their foot to go through. This is generally considered to be 100 mm, but I think 75 mm would be better. A suitable railing on at least one side is also essential, and this should be 1050 mm above the toe (the outside edge) of the tread.

If the distance between landings is 2700 mm, of which 150 mm can be expected to settle out, divide 2550 by 200, which equals 12.75. If you use 13 risers, the height of each step would then be 2550 divided by 13 to equal 196 mm. If you are uncomfortable with 13 steps you will have to use 12 or 14. Twelve would give a satisfactory rise of 212 mm for a steep stair, while 14 would give an easy rise of 182 mm. If you choose 14, and the run is to be 200 mm, you will need 200 times 14, or

2800 mm, for the stair plus another 1000 mm for a landing, for a total length of 3800 mm. The width should be a minimum of 800 mm.

A housed stringer is a first-class way to build a stairway. The stringer can be dimensional material or log. The treads and risers are dadoed about 15 mm into the stringer, glued into place and then slim wedges are driven in to keep them tight. Glue blocks are used between the tread and the riser for additional rigidity.

A stair horse is made by cutting the run and rise into a solid plank or log and fastening treads to this. The treads will have to be well fastened if they are to not squeak.

The stringers for these stairs can be hinged at the top. The treads are not strictly level until after the building has settled, and the stringer is expected to slide a little at the bottom.

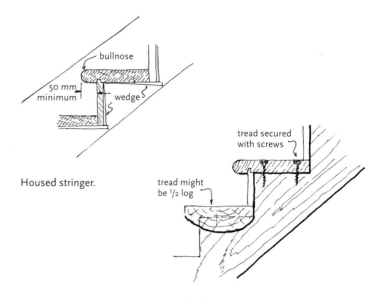

Housed stringer.

Stair horse (open stringer).

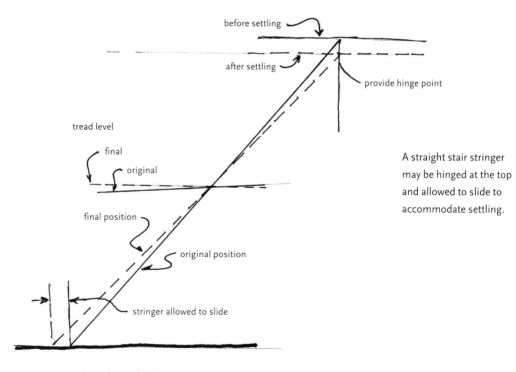

A straight stair stringer may be hinged at the top and allowed to slide to accommodate settling.

Straight or platform

Many people design spiral staircases but few actually build them because they are so difficult. This one was built by Daizen Log-Tech.

Spiral Stairs

Spiral stairs have been designed in a great variety of styles. They are most often constructed around a center post of some kind with pie-shaped treads radiating from this center. These stairs must be solidly made to be satisfactory. They are often made of welded steel. The layout follows the same formula as a straight stairway but, of course, the treads are tapered to the center.

This center post is the design used for the spiral staircase pictured above.

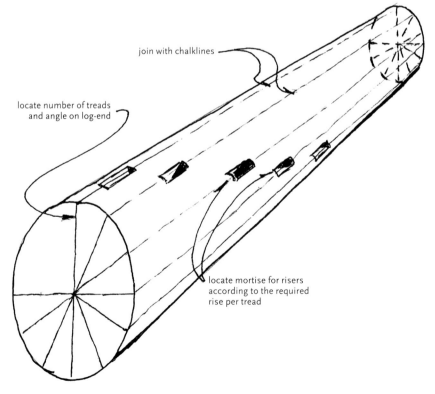

join with chalklines

locate number of treads and angle on log-end

locate mortise for risers according to the required rise per tread

Such a stairway might be constructed by drilling large holes, 125 to 150 mm in diameter, to a depth of 150 mm around a 400-mm (or larger) well-seasoned log. Well-seasoned, round risers can be epoxied into these holes, flattened on top and a tread added. The outer end can gain additional support from a rail of wood, metal or chain.

Settling for this spiral stair has to be considered. If the upright is secured at the bottom, there would have to be a long step at the top. This would be an extreme hazard. A long step at the bottom would not be much better. I like to put the upright center post on a screw jack at the bottom, with the top tread in its proper place. Instead of a long step at the bottom, build a platform that takes the place of a landing. This platform is approached before the steps are encountered. As the building settles and the steps are lowered, the platform can also be lowered.

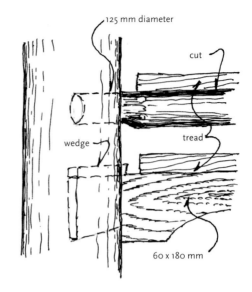

Two types of riser for a spiral staircase.

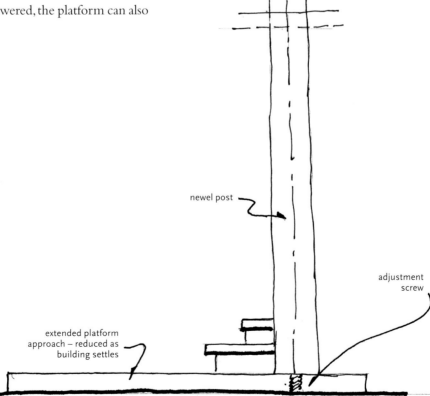

A screw jack under the center post can provide settling control for a spiral staircase. The platform approach would also have to be adjusted.

The first trial solar equipment (right) worked very well. I had enough energy to run lights, computers and VCRs for editing film.

Placing a settling board above the door (below).

I plan to use solar power here at Shanty Lake, but for power tools and construction needs I am using a small gasoline generator. With this I was able to make doors and window frames from 2 x 10 pine planks. The windows are single-glazed for the simple reason that I was able to go to a glass shop and get the glass cut right away. To use double-glazed units would require placing an order, then making the trek out again in a week or two to get them. Besides, I wanted to experiment with sizes.

It is always a temptation to cut in large windows. The added light was enough motive, for this even if there was not an interesting, active and changing field of view onto the lake. But large windows confound the integrity of the solid walls that have been built between me and the cold. I can go outside if I have a longing for the view. I am therefore happy with the small windows and next year I will add the sealed units and one more, slightly larger window on the lake side.

Be careful installing windows and doors. Plan the work well and do the cuts accurately. This will have direct dividends in comfort and appearance.

Starting the window cutout (above).

Fraser finishing the top of the keyway by hand (left). The cut shown here was made with a chainsaw after the walls were in place, and very dangerous. It is better done on the ground, before you assemble the walls.

CHAPTER 15

INTERIOR NEEDS

ELECTRICITY

I have mentioned electrical wire installation from time to time but I think there is still a little to be said.

Electricity, like cars, packaging, industrial waste, drift nets and loud music, is not in itself (with the exception of drift nets and loud music) a bad thing. Like all these things that we use every day, it is the amount of use that is important. Obviously we cannot sustain present-day population levels without the use of external power sources. We are not going to abandon our use of electricity, but we can, as a preparation for the almost inevitable crisis, learn to limit our consumption and develop alternate facilities.

What better place than in the planning stage of a log home to review your actual needs and to install accordingly. The essential needs in any house are light and heat, which may or may not be most reasonably supplied by electricity. You can cook and heat a house with wood or other fuels, but when houses become numerous, this can cause atmospheric problems. Other fuels, such as propane or natural gas, are possible alternatives, depending on where you live, and the installation of a methane generator might be a possibility if you own a farm. With recently improved technology, solar and wind power are also realistic alternatives. Electricity is really necessary only for devices, and although many of these certainly enhance our lives, many we might be much better off without.

So, install a service of adequate size, and I think this might be limited to a 100-amp service, and employ discretion in its use. The electrical plan should show the location of fixtures and switches and how they are to be connected. Additionally, you will find it advantageous to detail the actual routing of the wires as they will be placed in the walls.

Electrical wires can be led from below the floor to the second log through a drill hole which, in turn, should be large enough to allow easy access. When the second log has been fitted, drill through to the underside from

Normal electrical installation

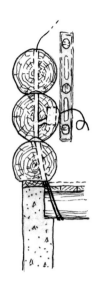

Cut electrical box recess into second log and drill access hole at an downward angle so that the wire will go in easily. Mark the line so that the hole can be drilled in the next log if required.

Remove second round and complete the hole in the first round by drilling at an angle to miss the foundation.

With second round in place, drill through it and first round about 20 mm.

the centerline on top with a drill diameter of 30 to 40 mm. Drill into the bottom log far enough to be able to locate the spot when the second log has been removed, then drill on through the first log at an angle that will just miss the inside of the foundation wall. If the hole is to be continued on up the wall, mark the line location on the side of the log and note the distance to the center of the hole. When the next log has been placed, extend the line and locate the drill center, then drill down to meet the previous drill hole. By this means, a continuing passage can be placed all the way up the wall.

When the level of the outlet has been reached, drill an intercept hole about 30 mm in diameter at a down slope, then cut out the recess for the receptacle. I like to make the cuts for the faceplate at right angles to the log. Many people scarf off a flat space for this, which is a bit quicker. This is strictly a matter of choice. Now place a piece of strong cord in the hole so that your electrician can easily attach the wire.

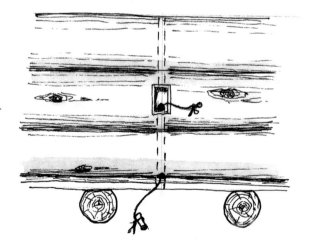

Place a strong pull cord or wire in the access hole for the use of the electrician.

Partitions

Partitions in a log house should, I think, be kept to the very minimum. They can also be made of logs. However, in a small house log partitions may take up too much room, and there are places where framed partitions serve a very useful purpose, such as a plumbing wall. A good plan is to divide the main areas with log partitions and the lesser divisions with framed walls. This way, the living room, kitchen and dining room might be in one area, while bedrooms and bathroom are in the other.

When log partitions are an extension of an

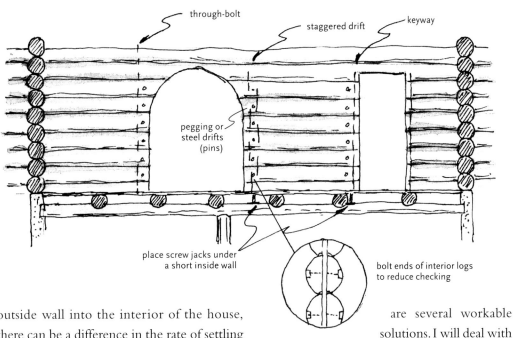

through-bolt

staggered drift

keyway

pegging or
steel drifts
(pins)

place screw jacks under
a short inside wall

bolt ends of interior logs
to reduce checking

Screw jacks under
interior walls can keep
them in place while the
exterior wall settles.
These log-ends must be
well keyed or pinned.

outside wall into the interior of the house, there can be a difference in the rate of settling between the two sections. This need not be a large concern because they will eventually reach the same state. In the meantime, though, log-ends should not be left free standing. If you have this situation in your building, the log-ends should be retained with a key piece or else be thoroughly pegged. If a cross wall has two doorways in it, the logs between the doors will shrink and fall away more quickly than the end portions. To regulate this, place screw jacks under the floor to keep the log-ends up tightly and lower the wall again as the extremities shrink.

Framed partitions can be built for most of the divisions in the house, although I prefer to keep these to a minimum. There are two things that you will have to attend to. The house will settle and the partition must be built in such a way that it can telescope, or move. For the same reason, the partition cannot be fitted or fastened to the curved logs of the wall. With these two points in mind, there are several workable solutions. I will deal with the most popular first.

Frame the partition from a bottom plate to a height just above the top of the door. This should leave a space of 400 to 500 mm from the top of the frame to the underside of the decking of the second floor. Frame the top section wider than the bottom section and leave ample settling space in between. The top piece must be wide enough to slip over the lower section (see 152A: End view). For a ceiling height of 2700 mm, that space should be 170 mm. The top section will have the additional width of the finish material that is to be used on the bottom part.

In at least two places, put bridging between the studs on the lower section. This should be about 600 mm below the top plate. Drill for a dowel (40 mm) that will be secured to the top section of the partition and free to slide through the top plate of the lower section and on through the bridge you just put between the studs. This will keep the partition wall

Framed partition wall. Settling space can be at the top of a partition wall. I would much rather key the partition to the logs with a central key than to cut in two slots for the sheathing.

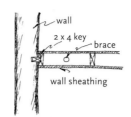

wall
2 x 4 key
brace
wall sheathing

Top view

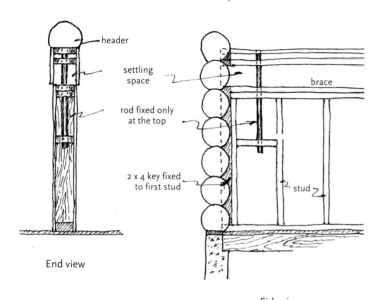

header

settling space

rod fixed only at the top

2 x 4 key fixed to first stud

brace

stud

End view

Side view

The preferred method for joining the partition to the logs is with a housed block, leaving the logs intact.

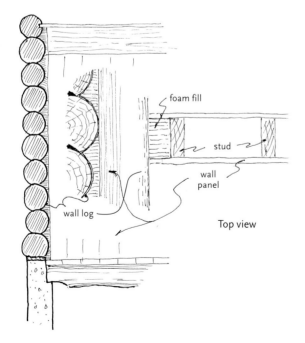

foam fill

stud

wall panel

wall log

Top view

solidly upright while still free to settle with the building.

At the wall end, a common practise is to cut two grooves into the log wall, one on either side of the first stud. The stud is fastened to the log wall through vertical slots so that it will not hang up, and the partition wall covering, or sheathing, is entered into the grooves cut into the log wall.

I very much dislike this system for most applications. First, it mutilates the wall and the room layout cannot be changed or altered afterward. My second objection is that it gives me an uncomfortable feeling. A solid and honest wall has been insulted by the intrusion of this less important or even trivial function. In some locations, such as a bathroom partition, this would be acceptable, but in most other locations it is not.

I will go to considerable effort to avoid this problem and the system I use is as follows: Place the first stud of the partition wall about 50 mm away from the log wall. Cut wood blocks that are the same width as the stud and fit them between the stud and the log wall. The grain of the wood for these blocks should be placed horizontally. The blocks should not be fastened permanently to either the stud or the wall but be allowed free movement after they have been caged in place by the wall covering. The wall covering of sheathing will, of course, extend the 50 mm past the first stud until it encounters the log wall.

On one building that is very well finished, the owners simply stuffed these spaces with colored cloth. It worked for them, but I do not think it would be my choice. I mention it only to indicate that you are indeed free to use your imagination. Blocks cut from foam and painted a suitable color are another possibility.

Think well on this before you take your chainsaw to the wall that you have built with such care and diligence.

Partitions can be built with many kinds of materials besides plywood and plaster board.

Solid planking that is pegged, slabs, cloth, bark and small poles are just a few that come to mind. When the house is to be used as a full-time residence, as most log houses are, you need to consider the long-term effect of the material you use. Give some thought to how you will feel about the materials some years hence.

FIREPLACES

A log house need not have a fireplace, but it is much better with one. We all know that a fireplace is one of the most inefficient ways to heat a house. But on long, dark winter nights or end-of-season evenings that need cheer as well as heat, inefficiency is rarely so well rewarded.

Fireplaces can be a lot of fun to build and, after all, radiant heat does work. People are often reluctant to build something as heavy as a fireplace, but since you were able to build a log house, the chances are very good that you will be able to build the fireplace too.

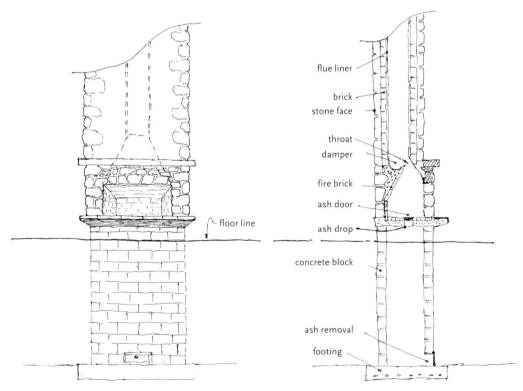

floor line

flue liner
brick
stone face
throat
damper
fire brick
ash door
ash drop
concrete block
ash removal
footing

The essential parts of a standard fireplace with a raised hearth. There are many books devoted to the building of fireplaces. It is a good experience.

Much of the anxiety can be removed if you use a fireplace form. A fireplace form is a manufactured, hollow metal form around which the masonry is constructed. There are also several books on fireplace construction available.

Build a substantial footing at the time the foundation is poured or built, and use plenty of steel in it. The footing should be 300 mm wider than the fireplace plan, or more if there is any question about the load-bearing ability of the soil. If you have a full basement, you can build a support up to the level of the hearth with concrete blocks. This will be a hollow structure and should have a small, cast-iron door for the removal of ashes.

The hearth will be a solid, reinforced concrete slab and have an ash-drop door in the center. The fireplace can now be constructed of concrete block and faced with stone, or it may be built entirely of stone, or, for that matter, brick. If you are not using a fireplace form, a temporary one can be made of plywood. Gather a good supply of rock: about twice as much as you think will be enough to do the job. I like uncut, rounded river rock, but I also like rubble rock and cut granite. Be sure that the type of rock is solid and not porous — volcanic rock may absorb water and shatter or even explode when it is heated.

Place the rock with a Portland cement mortar. The same rules for stonework apply here as for foundation work: keep the rock level from front to back and break the joints. A firebrick liner is necessary for the firebox. These are special fire-resistant bricks and a special mortar is used to place them. Install them onto the bottom, back and sides of the firebox. Do a neat job and use a very thin mortar line.

The chimney can be built the same way as the rest of the fireplace or you can use a form similar to the one described under foundations: a wire cage in two sections that can be moved up as required.

If you have not used stonework on the foundation and you feel that you need some practise, this might well be a good time to build the outdoor barbecue that you were planning anyway. Right! Now tackle your fireplace with confidence and enjoy it for years to come.

There have been questions about the environmental impact of large numbers of wood-burning devices in a community. This is indeed a valid question where, because of high fuel costs, some communities in extremely cold climates feel that they have to supplement their electric or oil heat with wood. In such a climate, a cold-weather inversion can trap the woodsmoke residue in the area, with more damage to the community than to the general

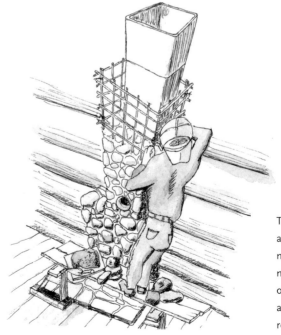

The way I like to build a stone chimney. A movable grid form can make a stonemason out of almost anyone. Use a form made of 6–8 mm rod for a guide.

environment. I doubt that the smoke from fireplaces would have any overall impact. All smoke should be reduced or eliminated, but I think there are far more worthy candidates for our immediate attention than fireplaces.

PLUMBING

Plumbing in a log house will be the same as plumbing in any other kind of house. Plumbing is simply a matter of getting fresh water in and distributing it and getting waste water out.

Since indoor plumbing and bathrooms have been in general use (and I can easily remember when most people did not have these things), they have had considerable impact on the environment. The impact has not all been bad; we have gained a lot in health and knowledge in those countries whose economies have allowed the general population to take advantage of these facilities. On the other hand, we have done more damage than we may realize in that we now export our pollution to rivers, lakes, ocean and the atmosphere. Most people feel that there is little they can do about this except feel bad and turn off the news.

For log builders undertaking a new project in a new location, the opportunity exists to do the most effective thing that anyone can do. You can choose not to contribute to the destruction of our environment. Limit the amount of water used; investigate the possibility of using solar energy to heat water; use a composting toilet or, at least, a low-flush toilet; compost and recycle other waste; and treat or filter waste water so that contaminants are not turned loose on the land. Unrealistic pipe dream? Not really. These measures may be inconvenient at times, but they offer practical alternatives. Most of us are not in a position to regulate the world, but the greatest freedom of all is that we are still largely free to regulate ourselves.

Plumbing, like electrical wiring, should be well planned in advance. If there is access under the floor, water pipes are reasonably simple. If the house is on a concrete slab, these pipes, or a space for them, will have to be placed in the concrete before the building begins. Water pipes can all come through the floor. Drain pipes can do the same except for vent stakes, which may have to be planned through a closet or cupboard if there is no framed partition handy. Water pipes to the second floor should have a loop or offset to relieve settling stress, and drain pipes can have slip joints installed. Obtain information on the building code regulations that apply locally and plan accordingly.

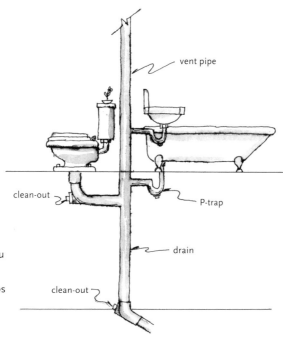

Plumbing is getting water in (to where you want it) and getting waste out. Use P-traps instead of S-traps.

HEATING AND COOLING

Other than the aforementioned fireplace, you have the choice of several heating alternatives: wood, electricity, gas, oil or solar heat.

When I lived in a very cold climate, I had the house designed so that all possible space could be closed off in the dead of winter and it was necessary to heat only the essential and protected space. I liked that because it gave a warm and secure feeling to the winter, and opening up the house became part of the ceremony of spring. Now we use a combination of wood heat and electric heat. Still, the best way to save fuel is to have a well-built house that is as small and well insulated as possible.

A stone-faced chimney can be an alternative to a fireplace, and a wood-burning stove heats more efficiently than a fireplace. If the stove has a stonework platform to sit on and a stone wall behind it, it can have a very pleasing appearance.

Stone can also be cool in the summer. Air conditioning is totally unacceptable to me because it is environmentally destructive from every point of view. Cooling can be accomplished by attention to ventilation. One of the main design considerations for this is to have the space as unobstructed as possible. Contrary to what might seem natural, a large vent opening should be on the side of the house away from the prevailing summer wind, for instance, up at the gable end. A smaller opening would be on the windward side. This configuration creates a low pressure within the upper house that draws in fresh air. My son built such a house where he lives near one of the desert areas in Australia. He arranged the air intake between stone walls on the lower level. The interior of the house was cool even when the daytime temperatures reached 110 degrees F.

Roof overhang can also be a factor. I always recommend a substantial overhang, but the angle of that overhang should be considered. Remember when I talked about site evaluation and recording the angle of the sun in summer and winter in Chapter 3? Use this information in your design so that the windows are shaded from the sun in the summer and exposed to the sun in winter. If you are not able to locate your windows and skylights to accommodate this, sometimes you can alter the vertical angle of the window to advantage. For example, a window that is sloped in at the bottom will be shaded for a long period of the day.

Lighting

The electric wires are all in and your next concern is the light fixtures for your log house. Certainly there is a variety of such things available and anyone who has built their own house would have no trouble choosing fixtures that demonstrate their good taste. But here again is an opportunity for skill and imagination if you decided to make all the lighting fixtures yourself. This will take a little time, but they do not all have to be installed at once and the final result will be gratifying.

At the same time that you are designing and making light fixtures, you might integrate the design for the hardware needed in and around the building. Blacksmithing has become a popular industry within the last few years, so help and information is more readily available than it was even a short time ago. It is therefore possible to have the work done locally or, better yet, learn to do the work yourself. Hinges, door pulls, light fixtures, railings, brackets and gates are only a few of the articles that might be undertaken. The list could go on and the activity may continue long after the house has been completed.

Light fixtures you can build. Let your skill and imagination run riot.

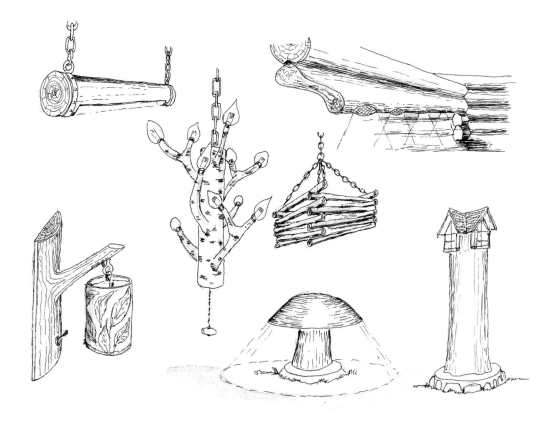

Walls

Clean and finish the walls on the outside and inside of the building. If you were able to complete the building and put the roof on within one season, there should be very little cleaning and preparation to be done on the walls.

Check each log for mechanical damage, bark or high knots and remove these either with hand tools or an angle grinder. Check the log-ends too to see if they are all cut, shaped or sanded the way you wish. Next, if the logs are not weathered, you need only wash them with a stiff bristled brush and let them dry. If the logs have been badly weathered, you can use oxalic acid or bleach to regain a lighter color. In very bad cases, the logs may have to be sanded or even sandblasted, although this last remedy is a bit drastic and can damage the appearance of the building if too coarse a sand is used.

Make sure that the logs are dry before you put any varnish or sealing type of finish on them. Applying a sealer too early can create a greenhouse environment under the finish, which will encourage the growth of stain, bacteria or fungus. If such a thing occurs, it will take a great deal of work to remove it. If some protection is needed while the logs are drying, use linseed oil or a mixture of water and borax.

When you are convinced that the moisture content of the logs is low enough, you can apply a finish. In many instances, the very best finish is to do nothing more than to clean the logs well. If the house is in an exposed location, you can apply a product such as Sikens Cetol or a CWF product. New products are always coming on to the market and you should check with suppliers to find out what is available. Any sealer you use should be resistant to sunlight and contain an ultraviolet screen. I have found that boiled linseed oil with an ultraviolet screen added will do as good a job as most products. You might want to place a few short logs in an exposed position and experiment with a variety of applications.

For the interior, use a coat of boiled linseed oil followed by a coat of low gloss varnish or synthetic finish. Such a finish is easy to dust or clean and will last a long time.

SHANTY LAKE

THE INTERIOR

Now that Knotingham is finished, I can welcome friends and family. Log buildings provide excellent acoustics, partly because the walls have no hard angles.

I have to confess that I did not drill for electrical when I disassembled Knotingham. I can see where I am going to pay for this in the near future. The house is off the grid, as they say, and I will use solar power to generate electricity. The wires and outlets will, however look about the same and I totally refuse to have wires nailed to the walls. I will have to crawl around under the building and drill up to intercept box cutouts, remove door frames and access the switches. Roof wiring can be done in a normal way, at least until after the ceiling material has been put up. Fortunately, the wiring will be minimal.

Partitions are not extensive here. One wall across the building is where the tie beam joins the two long sides of the building. This is hung from the beam with enough space left at the bottom to allow for settling. It is held in place by lag bolts into the floor. They can be taken up as required. Another partition will be made up of closets between the two bedrooms and this can just sit on the floor with an adequate space at the top. Even if I were putting in more permanent partitions, I would not cut the walls. I can visualize the floor plan for this house changing often and I would not like to do anything to inhibit that expression.

I do not have any plan to build a fireplace in this house. In the first place it would take too much room and it would heat less efficiently than a good wood stove. I do have a stone pad under the heater and next summer, I will make a stone back panel to go behind. The chimney is a stainless, insulated unit. It seems quite good and has done the job to date. A masonry chimney would be nice but again it would use valued space.

Plumbing does not exist. I plan to build a wash house separate from the building with a composting toilet and a gray-water sump to take care of bath water. At present I carry in water from the lake and carry out waste water. About four gallons a day is enough. But then I have spent a certain amount of time sailing on the ocean and I have learned to economize on the use of water. A guest house is not permitted to have a sink (according to township regulations), but if it were, the gray-water system should handle that also.

Modern solar equipment has gained in efficiency and popularity in the last few years. There are panels that produce 50, 75 or 90 watts that are guaranteed for twenty-five years. Along with batteries, inverters and regulators, one can install near-normal service for less than it would cost to have a pole line built to the house, and there will be no monthly hydro bills to pay. It is not practical to use solar power for heating or cooking and they still recommend propane for refrigerators. This may change before the allotted twenty-five years has elapsed. To date, propane has been practical for cooking and lighting.

This is the inside of the window Fraser and I made. It overlooks the lake.

CHAPTER 16

FINISHING TOUCHES

Strange as it may seem, it is the final details that make a house unique. These finishing jobs will be the railings, the rooflines, barge boards and window trim, and auxiliary structures such as a barbecue shelter, picnic table, benches, stonework, ironwork and glass work, as well as the landscaping and blending of the building with the site.

RAILINGS

Railings are an important part of a building and add considerably to the overall appearance. For most log buildings these will be made of natural materials selected for the purpose. This is not to say that other materials may not be suitable. Wrought-ironwork and manufactured wood materials can be very suitable, depending on the statement that you wish to make.

Natural wood railings are the most usual kind and many methods have been employed to make them firm. I have illustrated one way but many other possibilities exist. I am sure that you will have no trouble fixing on a system that will be satisfactory. More to the point, exterior beams and railings must be under the roof. Some builders have extended these out well beyond the protection of the roof and their work is soon destroyed.

Posts are best bolted to the log floor-joists or held to the floor with heavy metal brackets. The top rail can be placed with a post notch and the bottom rail secured with metal fasteners or tenons. The rail should be a minimum of 1075 mm high and the uprights should be no further than 100 mm apart. Horizontal or diagonal rungs are not as safe as upright ones because small children might climb up on them.

The usual practice is to drill holes of about 40 or 50 mm in diameter into the top and bottom rails to receive the uprights. These uprights will be cut to length and tapered to fit. A better job can done by cutting a rabbet into the rails, scarfing the uprights to fit and gluing a spacer block between them. Uprights made in this manner will not rotate.

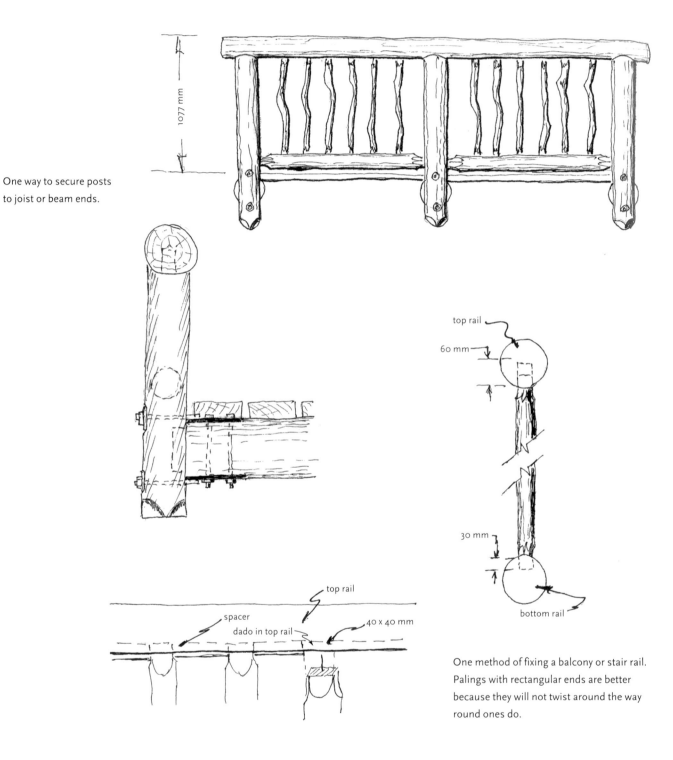

1077 mm

One way to secure posts
to joist or beam ends.

top rail

60 mm

30 mm

bottom rail

top rail

spacer

dado in top rail

40 x 40 mm

One method of fixing a balcony or stair rail.
Palings with rectangular ends are better
because they will not twist around the way
round ones do.

Shelters

Barbecue shelters and picnic shelters can be made to almost any size. They can be post-and-beam construction or part round-log construction. This is where your skill with post notches and fitting mortise and tenon joins will pay off. The picnic table that is illustrated has been built many hundreds of times. The first one of these was designed as an exercise in square-notch cutting. The project still serves that purpose but it also makes a good picnic table and a place to relax. Benches of log or stone can be used in the garden or on a porch.

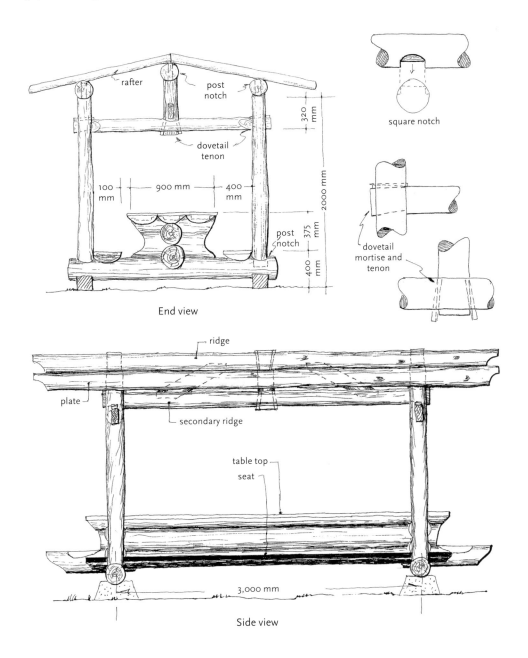

This popular picnic table has an optional roof.

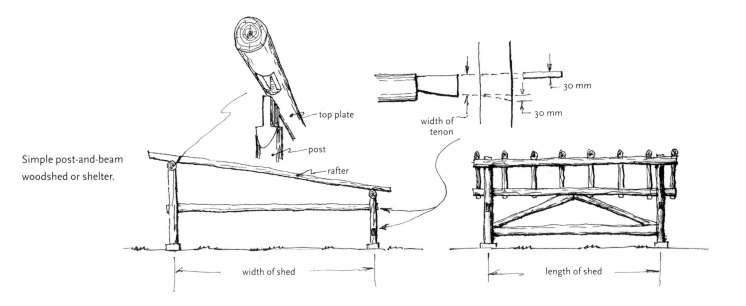

top plate

post

rafter

30 mm

30 mm

width of tenon

Simple post-and-beam woodshed or shelter.

width of shed

length of shed

FURNITURE

Build in as much furniture as is reasonably possible while you are building the house. I think it should be feasible to supply most of your needs in this manner. The house needs to be designed with this approach in mind, so that building in benches or tables is not overlooked as you go along and the requirements are all identified. Two of the advantages of built-in, free-standing furniture are that you can sweep under it without hindrance and you will not have to move it.

Benches can be placed near the entrance of

Build in as much furniture as you reasonably can.

Built-in table.

Built-in seat.

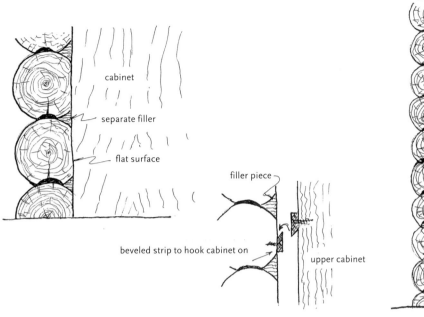

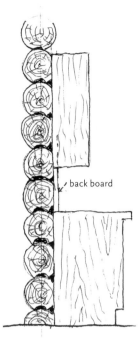

cabinet

separate filler

flat surface

filler piece

beveled strip to hook cabinet on

upper cabinet

back board

Placing kitchen cabinets. Upper cabinets can be attached to the wall at one point with hanger board.

your house, kitchen counters and tables can be extended from the wall, logs can be placed to support light fixtures, and coat racks, shelves, cabinets and even beds can be built in. This approach may not meet every need, but it can be used for many functions and should be given consideration.

Stained-glass work at doors or upper windows seems to fit with the logs. Perhaps it is because the bright colors contrast with the reserved shades of the wood. Whatever the reason, these windows add a note of cheer that never goes amiss.

Kitchen cabinets should be of solid wood construction and built in a material and style that you will be able to live with for a long time. The lower cabinets can be free standing and a splashboard up the back will supply a location for electrical outlets and pipes, if necessary. The wall behind the cabinet may be cut flat so that the units will fit close to the wall, or a skirting can be applied in much the same manner as with a partition wall (see Chapter 15).

The upper units can be hung from one log. Use a 150-mm board and rip it lengthwise with a 45-degree miter cut. One half of this board can be secured to the wall log and the other half properly located on the cabinet. To place the cabinet, simply hook one strip over the other and screw it into place. A spacer piece will have been placed at the bottom to keep everything plumb.

GUEST HOUSE

If you are fortunate enough to have the space, time and material, you may want to undertake a practice project before you start your serious house. Such a project can be of any scale, depending on your space. It can be any size: a doghouse, a playhouse for children, a sauna or bathhouse or a substantial guest house. A project such as a guest house can not only serve as a means to hone your building skills and refining techniques, but it can also become an on-site residence while the main house is being built. You may, at present, have every reason to feel totally confident of your skill and ability, but it is always possible to learn more, and as stated before, one house is never enough! By building a practise house first, you will go a long way toward building your best log house.

LEARNING MORE

In line with building the best log house, I must, in all sincerity, suggest that it will be in your best interest to attend a course in log-building construction before you undertake your project. I also expect that my recently released series of video instruction, *Building With Logs*, will be a great help to the beginning builder (see Appendix). This can be part of the investigation and preparation that would be part of any project. The time required to do this will be repaid in time saved on the house and the cost will be repaid many times over, not only in direct savings of time and material, but you will build a better house with a minimum of error.

Taking a log-building course has got to be the best and quickest way to get experience, and even experienced builders can benefit from this opportunity to experiment with ideas before they get into the final project.

THE GREAT ADVENTURE

You are ready and prepared to build a log house: you have the site, the plans, the materials and the skills. You are ready to give the undertaking your best effort. To my way of thinking, there are three broad groups of log buildings and your project will fall within one of these groups: commercial buildings, professionally built off-site buildings and personal log houses built by the owner. They are all acceptable building forms and I have no quarrel with any of them. Two of these forms have been around for a long time and only one is a newcomer to the stage, the professional off-site building method.

Commercial buildings may be large or small but they are most often built by a contractor rather than the owner, and their function is less personal than other buildings. Included here are hotels, lodges, restaurants, specialty shops, offices and a host of other applications.

Standard, "modern" log houses are professionally built off-site by a building yard, delivered to the owner's property, re-erected and finished. This is a system of building that emerged in the mid-seventies and has become an accepted and almost standard way of building.

The third class of building, the kind I have been investigating in this book, is a personal log house. This kind of house is always built by the owner, his family and friends. The house may be very large or it may be very small. It may be built with extreme accuracy or it may be a little on the casual side. The essential ingredient is that it is an undertaking of the spirit. It is a statement, if only in the mind of the builder, about his feelings and beliefs in respect to building, dwelling on the earth, the environment and perhaps many other things. In this he is connected to the many others who have also undertaken this same challenge.

At this point I should simply wish you well and end this book. Indeed, that is what I will do, because if you have persevered to this point, you are probably very determined and you will build your house. I will, however, warn you that when you have overcome each and every obstacle that you encounter, and you are finally installed in your house and ready to put your feet up and contemplate a job well done, be very careful before you part with this house.

Certainly you may want to build more and to do a better job each time. This is natural and commendable, but this first house will come to mean more and more to you as time goes by. You will find that you put a lot of yourself into it and you will, to some degree, lose that part of yourself if you leave this house, for whatever reason. Such a course may be unavoidable and it will not be a disaster; we have all experienced this feeling to some extent. This first house has more meaning than many things and it should be treated with care.

In this respect, I would offer one other piece of advice. This little advice may be very well known to you already, and if that is the case then we have reached a degree of understanding. I have already said this before, but it stands repeating.

Take joy in your work. Work with discre-

tion but work hard. It may be only once in your lifetime that you are able to do this. Be aware that you are directly contributing to your own welfare and experience and every bit of the process should be savored and recorded in your mind. I do not recommend that you expose yourself to mindless or unnecessary danger, but growth requires a proportional degree of risk and adventure. This is a great adventure.

SHANTY LAKE

AN ECOLOGICAL HOUSE

Knotingham sits serene among the birches, in harmony with the environment.

Finishing touches are still on the waiting list. At the top of the list is a screened-in porch/deck/woodshed on the end of the building. Snow here does not come drifting lazily down: it comes hurtling in like the prop wash of a Lancaster bomber. It becomes plastered onto the side of the building, trees or anything else that is out there. A porch would protect the east end of the building and keep the wood dry.

Other outbuildings would make life easier. Pioneering seems to mean first to survive and second to make your life and surroundings more convenient. I would like to add a third characteristic of pioneering: do so without harm.

The project at Shanty Lake is not so much a demonstration as it is an experiment. Can a person move into a relatively remote and undisturbed site, create a comfortable and livable condition comparable to the standard of living enjoyed by the other members of this society? In addition, can this be done without changing the nature of the site to the point where its balance is unstabilized?

The natural balance has been upset before. I learned that this area was once covered with large cedar trees. There are scattered mounds of moss that upon investigation reveal great cedar stumps. The area was heavily logged but has regrown with hardwoods in the last one hundred years. Now there are no cedar trees of any size. The site has obviously been changed and may be in a process of recovery that might take many years.

The first necessity was a road, cleared to the width that would allow a usable surface with room for drainage and snow removal. Earlier settlers used horses. With narrower vehicles and no need for snow removal their roads could be half the width of ours. However, horses need hay and a lot more land needed to be cleared to provide that fuel. The process of clearing for the road did not appear to change the characteristics of the area: drainage was provided without erosion or silting of the downstream areas.

There are still a few finishing touches to be done, including the trim on the door and windows.

The next step was clearing the building site. The site could be limited to the size of the footprint of the little house and enough room to turn the truck around. This would be possible if the building were done with a truck-mounted crane or similar device. I cleared a larger area to use as a building yard where I had room to use wheeled machines. For my convenience I cleared this area to have a small working space with dry ground. Drying out this amount of land changes the immediate area, but does not appear to have affected the surroundings. Time may tell a little in this regard because, as we are slowly coming to understand, whatever we do causes a ripple effect that may have consequences far into the future. The area does not seem to be in any hurry to change – it's still wet.

The walls for Ardea, the big house at Shanty Lake, are all in place. I hope to finish the roof this summer and move in sometime in the fall of 2001.

So far, I think our activity has caused no harm. The more difficult challenge is to avoid pollution of the site by sewage, spilled oil, abandoned machinery and all the attendant shards of habitation. However, this is a challenge I am determined to meet. I am enchanted by all the birds and animals who make this their home and in their turn help to keep it in balance. I would be ashamed to do less.

Glossary

axe pattern shape and size of axe for special applications: e.g., swamping, hewing, battle, camping

bevel angle or slope applied to the edge of a material

bight loop or bend in a line or rope

bow (of a log) the direction of the bend or belly of a log

cap log the log that will cover (or cap) the ends of the floor joists; often the last log on the wall

chainsaw mill chainsaw attachment intended to guide the saw to produce lumber

collar-tie the horizontal beam between principal rafters above tie-beam height

come-along a hand-operated winch

corbels short supporting logs

course a continuous horizontal row of materials: brick, shingles, shakes, stones

cove a concave groove cut lengthway in a log

crush (tab) short length of wood intended to collapse under weight

dado rectangular groove cut in log to accept dimensional lumber

drawknife heavy two-handed knife used to peel or shape wood

drip break groove cut under a bottom log to prevent water intrusion

EM SEAL the most efficient commercial product used to seal logs

fascia board placed around the edge of the roof to cover lower ends of rafters

froe tool used to hand-split cedar shakes

gasket seal commercial product used to seal joins

girt a short beam that joins two bents, which are frames that go across a building

gouge chisel curved chisel

grade beam foundation beam above ground supported by piers or piling

gray water used sink or bath water

half-log a log split in two

hammer-beam a component of a truss

hang-up log or timber that is held up unintentionally by another part of the building

J-bolt anchor bolt used in foundations

key stock material used to fit in a groove in log end to prevent displacement

keyway groove in log ends

king-post upright central component of a truss

lap-notch two timbers fitted end-to-end

load-out loading of materials for shipment

log dogs devices used to keep logs in place

miter angular cut on end of log

mortise recess hole cut into wood, usually rectangular, designed to receive another part, such as a tenon

outrigger log placed outside wall line as a plate log

overscribing scribing a groove larger than the gap in anticipation of shrinkage

parbuckle the action of rolling a log with a line

parging covering masonry with mortar or grout to produce a smooth surface

peavey tool used to roll logs

peeling spud heavy tool used to peel logs

piece-on-piece style of building originating in Normandy where logs are shaped into posts with horizontal panels of short logs between the posts

pit house prehistoric house built in a pit with a roof added

plate log last log on wall from which roof line will originate

post-and-beam construction method with a framework of horizontal and upright beams

purlin a horizontal beam supporting rafters or boards

queen-post an upright component of a truss

rabbet groove in timber or log cut to receive the edge or tongue of another piece

recurve a line that curves under or backwards

scarf shallow miter on a log or timber

scarf board template for scarf layout

scoring shallow cut made across the grain of wood before cutting

scorp curved drawknife

scribe a line tracing a measurement from an original surface to a second surface

shake bolts block of wood from which (cedar) shakes are cut

sill log bottom log on house

skyline line suspended between two supports for the transport of material

sleepers timbers on or in the ground that support a load

slick large, chisel-like tool used for flatwork

soffit the undersurface of the rafters, outside the wall

spline a slim piece of wood keying two pieces together

spud tool for digging, prying or peeling

Starret divider scribing tool made by Starret Corporation

tang short end of carpenter's square

tenon a projecting piece of wood made to fit into a slot (mortise) on another piece of wood

through-bolt bolt extending through the height of the wall

tie beam lower cord of a truss

trenching (for services) digging a ditch for the installation of pipes, wires or other services

undercourse strip of tarred paper placed under each course of shakes on the roof

V-groove a groove in a log made with two cuts in the shape of a "V"

wall tent a tent that has low perpendicular walls

wracking leaning and twisting

METRIC CONVERSION

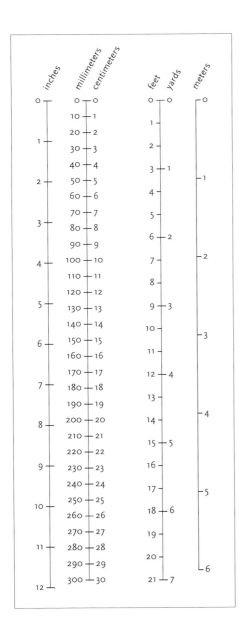

FORMULA FOR DETERMINING CIRCUMFERENCE OF A TREE

from Chapter Two

If looking for a tree with a diameter of 14 to 18 in, your calculations would look like this:

$$3.1416 (\Pi) \times 14 (\text{D}) = 44$$
$$3.1416 (\Pi) \times 18 (\text{D}) = 56$$

Make your knots at 44 and 56 in.

VOLUME MEASURE FOR LOGS

The cubic content of wood in a log is a measurement used for buying and selling the material. The wood content of a log was formerly expressed in board foot measurement (BFM). This is suited for measuring lumber but it is grossly in error when it is used to measure logs.

Because of this error, the forest industry moved to calculating the volume of a tree in cubic feet and the material was bought and sold for the actual wood content, using a hundred cubic feet as a basic unit. This is much more realistic for the log market, since many logs are not used strictly for the production of lumber. The universal acceptance of metric measurement required only a simple conversion to cubic meters. The following tables can be used for small volumes of logs, but the practice in large-scale production is to weigh the material and compare the weight to the cubic content by hand measuring.

HALF-VOLUME OF CYLINDERS IN CUBIC DECIMETERS

Radius (cm)	Length of log in meters									
	3	4	5	6	7	8	9	10	11	12
10	47	63	79	94	110	126	141	157	173	188
11	57	76	95	114	133	152	171	190	209	228
12	68	90	113	136	158	181	204	226	249	271
13	80	106	133	159	186	212	239	265	292	319
14	92	123	154	185	216	246	277	308	339	369
15	106	141	177	212	247	283	318	353	389	424
16	121	161	201	241	281	322	362	402	442	483
17	136	182	227	272	318	363	409	454	499	545
18	153	204	254	305	356	407	458	509	560	611
19	170	227	284	340	397	454	510	567	624	680
20	188	251	314	377	440	503	565	628	691	754
21	208	277	346	416	485	554	623	693	762	831
22	228	304	380	456	532	608	684	760	836	912
23	249	332	415	499	582	665	748	831	914	997
24	271	362	452	543	633	724	814	905	995	1086
25	295	392	491	584	687	785	884	982	1080	1178

To determine the volume of a log from this table, first read off the half-volumes corresponding to the top radius and length and the butt radius and length of the log. The addition of these two volumes will equal the volume of the log in cubic decimeters. Division by 1000 gives the volume in cubic meters. Half-volume of cylinders has been used to bypass the need to add the volume of butt and top diameters together and then divide by two.

To work out the volume for any log use the following formula, where $\Pi = 3.1416$; r = radius (½ diameter); and L = length.

$$\frac{\Pi r^2 \text{ [top] x L} + (\Pi)r^2 \text{ [butt] x L}}{2}$$

For example, for a log 8 m long with 20 cm top diameter and 30 cm butt diameter, the calculations look like this:

$$\frac{3.1416 \text{ x } (.10 \text{ x } .10) \text{ x } 8 + 3.1416 \text{ x } (.15 \text{ x } .15) \text{ x } 8}{2}$$

$$= \frac{.251328 + .565488}{288} = \frac{.816816}{2}$$

$$= .408408$$

Therefore, this log has a volume of .409 cubic m.

By table:
10-cm line (126) + 15-cm line (283)
  = 409 = .409 cubic m.

HALF-VOLUME OF CYLINDERS IN CUBIC FEET

Radius (inches)	Length of log in meters															
	10	12	14	16	18	20	22	24	26	28	30	32	34	36	38	40
4	1.7	2.1	2.4	2.8	3.1	3.5	3.8	4.2	4.5	4.9	5.2	5.6	5.9	6.3	6.6	7.0
5	2.6	3.3	3.8	4.4	4.9	5.5	6.0	6.5	7.1	7.6	8.2	8.7	9.3	9.8	10.4	10.9
6	3.9	4.7	5.5	6.3	7.1	7.9	8.6	9.4	10.2	11.0	11.8	12.6	13.4	14.1	14.9	15.7
7	5.4	6.4	7.5	8.6	9.6	10.7	11.8	12.8	13.9	15.0	16.0	17.1	18.2	19.2	20.3	21.4
8	7.0	8.4	9.8	11.2	12.6	14.0	15.4	16.8	18.2	19.6	20.9	22.3	23.7	25.1	26.5	27.9
9	8.8	10.6	12.4	14.1	15.9	17.7	19.4	21.2	23.0	24.7	26.5	28.3	30.0	31.8	33.6	35.3
10	10.9	13.1	15.3	17.5	19.6	21.8	24.0	26.2	28.4	30.5	32.7	34.9	37.1	39.3	41.5	43.6
11	13.2	15.8	18.5	21.1	23.8	26.4	29.0	31.7	34.3	37.0	39.6	42.2	44.9	47.5	50.2	52.8
12	15.7	18.9	22.0	25.1	28.3	31.4	34.6	37.7	40.8	44.0	47.1	50.3	53.4	56.6	59.7	62.8

To discover the volume of a log from this table, first read off the half-volumes corresponding to the top radius of the log and the butt radius of the log. Add these two volumes to obtain the log content in cubic feet.

To work out the volume for any log use the following formula, where $\Pi = 3.1416$; r = radius (½ diameter); and L = length.

$$\frac{\Pi r^2 \text{ [top] x L} + (\Pi)r^2 \text{ [butt] x L}}{144 \text{ x } 2}$$

For example, for a log 30 ft long with a 12-in top and a 18-in butt, the calculations look like this:

$$\frac{3.1416 \text{ x } (6 \text{ x } 6) \text{ x } 30 + 3.1416 \text{ x } (9 \text{ x } 9) \text{ x } 30}{144 \text{ x } 2}$$

$$\frac{3392.928 + 7634.088}{288}$$

$$\frac{11027.016}{288} = 38.28825$$

Therefore, this log has a volume of 38.3 cubic ft.

By table:
6-in line (11.8) + 9-in line (26.5)
= 38.3 cubic ft.

Numbers in italics refer to illustrations.

A

air-conditioning, 73, 205

Ardea, *13, 220. See also* Shanty Lake.

axe patterns, 82, 221

    swamping, 82, *83*, 98

axes, 98, 99, *100*, 110

B

balconies, *212*

bathrooms; *see* plumbing

building codes and standards, 50, 84, 134, 151, 174–175, 204

building time, estimating, 61–62

building trees; *see* trees

C

cap logs, 128, 152, 221

cedar, 25, 38, 108

cedar shakes, 174–175

chainsaw guides, 143, 180, 181

chainsaws, 98, 125

charts and tables,

    for determining log volume, 224–225

    for metric conversion, 223

chimneys, 72, 203. *See also* fireplaces.

circumference, formula to determine, 30, 223

codes, building; *see* building codes and standards

collar-ties, 221. *See also* trusses, collar-tie.

conservation, of forests, 33–34

construction methods,

    piece-on-piece, 135, *140*, 140–145

    pole frame, *35*

    post-and-beam, 36, 146–147, *162*, 222

    round-log, 134

    short-log, 145, *145*

    timber-frame, 35–36

corbels, *151*, 152, 221

cost worksheets, 68–75

costs, building, 61–66

cross-sections, *44, 52, 54. See also* plans.

cross-sleepers, 82–83

crush (tabs/sections), 124, *124*, 221

cypress, 25, 38

D

dead man anchors, *96*

design portfolios, 49–50

diameter, mean (midpoint), 28

door frames, 185–186, *186*

doors, 72, 123–125, 179, 183

Douglas fir, 25, 26, 38, 108

dovetail notches; *see* notches, dovetail

drafting equipment, 50, 51

drawknife, 93, 99, 221

drift pins, 124, 128

drip breaks, *38*, 84, *84*, *181*, 221

E

ecology, 19–21, 218–220

electrical, 197–198

    drilling for, 114, *115*, 122, 198

    installation of, 121–122, 176, *198*

    at Knotingham, 208

    plan for, 121, 197

    wall outlets, 121

    wiring for, 197–198

elevations, *43, 49, 50, 52, 52, 59. See also* plans.

EM SEAL, 115, 130, 221

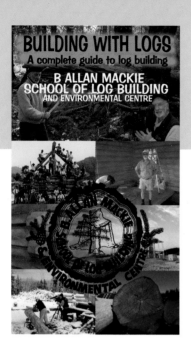

BUILDING WITH LOGS
On video cassette

This set of nine videos is a complete guide on how to build a log home. They give step-by-step instructions to build a log home shell. The latest building techniques are presented without sacrificing respect for nature.

TAPE 1: INTRODUCTION
This video tells you what you have to consider and prepare if you are going to work on your own log building. It also covers serious safety instructions.

TAPE 2: TOOLS & TERMS
Shows you what type of tools you will need and how to use them. It also explains the log building terms that you will need to know.

TAPE 3: HOUSE START
Shows you how to prepare your building site and how to set up temporary and permanent foundations.

TAPE 4: BASIC BUILDING
This teaches you how to practise for the first time and then gives you the complete procedure for laying out a log on the building.

TAPE 5: OTHER NOTCHES I
Step-by-step instructions for the blind dovetail notch, lock notch and square notch.

TAPE 6: OTHER NOTCHES II
Step-by-step instructions for the round notch, blind wall notch, dovetail notch and post notch.

TAPE 7: WALLS/WINDOWS & DOORS
Basic instructions for wall construction, openings for windows and doors and instruction on how to provide for electrical access.

TAPE 8: JOIST & BEAMS/ROOF SYSTEMS
All instructions on how to build second floors and post-and-beam roof systems.

TAPE 9: ROOF SYSTEMS II
Step-by-step detail on how to build roof trusses.

Set of nine videos: $400 CDN
Individual video: $50 CDN

HOW TO ORDER
All orders and inquiries for video, books and course information please contact:
B. Allan Mackie School of Log Building
c/o DAIZEN LOG-TECH LTD.
1285 Springhill Road, Parksville,
British Columbia, CANADA V9P 2G1
Phone: 250-248-0294
Fax: 250-248-6352
e-mail: log@daizen.com

More tapes are in production that will cover the finishing of log buildings, with one tape devoted to hand-built log buildings.

OTHER BOOKS
Building With Logs
Building With Logs in New Zealand
Log House Plans
Log Span Tables for Floor Joists, Beams and Roof Support Systems by B. Allan Mackie, Norman A. Read and Thomas M. Hahney
Notches of All Kinds: A Book of Timber Joinery